FLOATER FISHING

CARP IN DEPTH SERIES

Brian Skoyles
Chris Ball

Published by
Paisley-Wilde Publishing Ltd
1 Grosvenor Square, Sheffield S2 4MS

First published in 1991 by
Paisley-Wilde Publishing Ltd.
1 Grosvenor Square,
Sheffield S2 4MS

British Library Cataloguing in Publication Data

Brian Skoyles, Chris Ball,
Floater Fishing
1. Carp Angling
1 Title
799. 1'752

ISBN 1 871700 25 6

Produced, Typeset and Published by
Paisley-Wilde Publishing Ltd.

Printed by
Gibbons Barford Print Ltd.

DEDICATION

To all those surface feeding carp that have filled me with excitement, despair, frustration and fulfilment for twenty years and more. Long may they continue to do so.

Chris Ball

ACKNOWLEDGEMENTS

My grateful thanks to the following..........

Gary Bayes of Hook-Um Tackle who stocks and supplied me with many of the shop bought controllers mentioned in this book.

Peter Drennan who also supplied me with various controllers and different types of line to experiment with.

Geoff Kemp who for several years supplied me with some excellent flavours and base ingredients for my earlier floater cakes.

Last but not least Bill Cottam, friend, and Nutrabaits boss who has put my way many excellent oils, flavours, enhancers, and base ingredients that have continued to play an important part of my floater fishing.

Writing this book has involved me in examining my floater fishing over many years. As a result I would like to make special mention of the following................

Dave McMillan, for many years angling companion and close friend. Dave and I have shared many hundreds of hours floater fishing. My fishing has been better for it. Thanks mate!

A very special thank you to Jim Whitfield (sadly no longer with us) who had the foresight to create, in Emmotland, a fishery that for many years was the learning ground for much floater fishing and the provider of treasured memories too many to count. Also Margaret Whitfield: Maggie has continued to run Emmotland since Jim's untimely death and I've appreciated her continued friendship and involvement with the water.

Finally to the boss of the Skoyles household. Liz has helped enormously in the production of my share of this book with many hours of finger numbing word processing.

Very few can succeed on their own. I certainly can't. I owe a debt to many, and to those mentioned in particular.

To you all .... THANKS

Brian Skoyles.

CONTENTS

INTRODUCTION

This is silly. All the rest of the book is written and it was a relatively painless process.

We both agreed on a basic format after a discussion in a pub car park. and parted with scribbled notes on the back of envelopes.

We both have a passion for floater fishing and we both go back a long way, with many memories of fishing for carp on the top.

We both have our own favourite methods, baits etc., etc., so it wasn't necessarily going to be easy to co-write a book, but it has been - until now.

That's why it's so silly. How come a few words of introduction should prove so difficult?

What is actually in the book is easy. We decided to concentrate on three areas:

Tackle, including rigs and techniques.

Bait, the history and present thinking.

Approaching different waters.

All good, instructional stuff, or at least we hope so, but floater fishing is much more than tackle and technique. It's a very personal aspect of carp fishing.

You can see your quarry, in some cases, many times over the years. We both know some fish almost as friends, and within a little can judge how they will react to a particular situation.

Much of the fishing is at very close range. You can see and sense the fish's nervous reactions. Watch the tentative sucks and swirls as baits are tested. At times you struggle to hold the rod still, as the rod end exaggerates the trembling hand that waits those final seconds before the bait disappears and the strike is made.

You can't get enough of it. It's like a drug. The afternoon's work drags on and takes forever as you watch the clock on those beautiful summer days when you know the fish will be **ON TOP**.

So, we've had to compromise because we want this book to help you catch carp off the surface. We've spent a lot of our time writing how, rather than why, when in reality, it's the why that's more important.

We hope you enjoy the book, but more important we hope it helps you enjoy your surface fishing. Perhaps you are like us, already obsessed, or perhaps you are just getting started. Either way, we wish you tight lines and every success with your surface fishing.

Chris and Brian

BAIT

The floater angler has a wide variety of baits to choose from. Much has changed since the simple matchbox sized piece of crust was the normal, if not only, surface bait that the carp angler would use.

Having said that, the floater angler has a wide variety, it is interesting to chronicle how this variety has developed. Some of the more recent baits in particular have proved to be both outstanding and consistent. Bearing this in mind, we intend to take a look at the development of floater baits over the years and then concentrate on those that have proved to be the most effective.

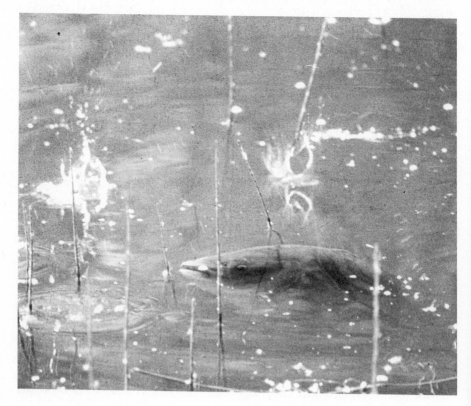

A LOOK BACK AT FLOATING BAIT DEVELOPMENT

Chris Ball

While Brian will take you through the modern part of floater fishing baits and their preparation, let me talk of the origins of this side of carp fishing, which we will find to be as old as the hills.

If we look at the fish itself, **the carp**, it is one of a few cyprinids that will happily feed on the surface, although it's a known bottom feeder or, should I say, it's better known for bottom feeding. The whole make up of a carp is geared towards effective bottom feeding, for when you look closely at a carp's mouth, with its extendible top membrane lip that is highly moveable, this, along with the sensitive barbels, four in all, gives it a system that is second to none. The sight of a carp foraging on the bottom will show you how superbly equipped our favourite species is for this kind of feeding. So why are they, at times, such avid surface feeders?

Here we have to look at the carp's habits and the like. I think I am right in saying that carp, probably more than most of their close relatives, just love to bask in the warm upper layers of water whenever possible. They will often sunbathe in groups, like we do on the beach, and if not disturbed will while away many hours, sometimes all day, (sounds great - might be good being a carp!). But with this kind of behaviour, opportunities to come across many a food item are presented to the fish. Don't run away with the idea that carp won't feed when they are holed up in this way. My experiences lead me to think that floater fishing in these circumstances is worthwhile.

So I believe this time spent on the surface, either just lying still or swimming, is one of the reasons why the carp recognises the opportunities of the odd tit-bit. Another point, have you ever noticed carp 'sucking' at the undersides of lily pads? It's the grubs and insects that they are having a go at. You don't see bream, tench or other bottom feeders do this often; if you spot the lilies shaking or moving upwards and you can see a dark shape close by, it will nearly always be a carp that's responsible. I remember once at Wraysbury watching a huge fish systematically working the pads for this haven of food. He was almost standing on his tail, in a vertical position, so to speak, to feed in this way. The sheer size of his mouth, as big as a medium sized orange, actually had enough suction to make the lily pad concave and dent as he searched the underside. Carp will maximise also on any fly hatches that naturally occur in the water, as well as chase small fry that are close to the surface.

This all adds up to give a picture of why carp feed on the surface and why, when a piece of bread is either seen or smelt, carp will know it's there and, second, will often investigate.

The origins of purposely fishing for carp on the surface go back many, many years. Look in 'B.B.'s' 'Confessions of a Carp Fisher' and you will see a whole chapter devoted to this one topic. 'B.B.' in fact, did not pen this piece, it was written by another long time carp angler, Flt. Lt. Burton. His chapter entitled 'Floating Bait Method' gives you all the basic methods that are still with us today. His observations on carp behaviour enabled him to make good catches with some big fish among them, especially creditable when you take into account the time of his experiments with floating bread. Naturally, there were other individuals (carp anglers) who were experimenting also but, in fairness, only very few had successfully succeeded in mastering this specialised technique.

It was Richard Walker's emergence in the late 1940's that gave hope to many. Dick had been successful in pioneering a method that had worked so well at one of his local waters. It was what he called 'margin fishing' for carp. I think it was Dick who first became aware that carp would feed in this way, and then successfully caught them.

From about 1932 onwards, Dick had regularly fished a pond which contained carp, and caught a number of them by the usual methods, the most effective of which was floating crust, cast well out on a greased line. The method was also used by many other anglers, since an angling club had the fishing rights of the pond, which was quite small. The quantity of bread crust cast upon its waters during the summer became considerable, and a great many carp were hooked, a few being landed. By 1935, the fish had become very crafty about floating bread. They would never touch the ordinary crust on a greased line; the nearest they came to doing this was to swirl violently close to it, repeating this until the sodden crust broke up and the hook sank. At a discreet interval afterwards, they would return and devour the pieces.

One or two were fooled by the old dodge of casting out a big crust attached to the line and having the hook concealed in a much smaller piece, but the whole business was obviously becoming less and less effective, even at night. This had, by then, become about the only time you could hope for a fish, mainly due to the increasing number of people who fished the water and who, like many anglers at the time, never really believed that carp could see, or detect vibrations on the bank; an attitude which, Dick thought, had not altered appreciably over the years.

During the summer of 1935, Dick spent several nights carp fishing and soon could not fail to observe that as soon as dusk had come and other anglers

Dick Walker - margin crust pioneer.

had packed up, the carp would come right in to the bank after crusts etc. They would even compete with the numerous rats for them, which Dick noticed was something comical. Late that summer it dawned on him that to throw a crust twenty yards out into the pool was rather stupid, when he had seen numerous carp take crusts within a couple of yards of where he sat.

If, at the time, he had read H. T.Sheringham's 'Coarse Fishing', written in 1912, Dick might have worked it out earlier. This is what Sheringham had to say: 'At dusk, the fish begin to roam in search of food, and in a lake they will cruise about among the weeds and reeds close inshore. Often, just at dusk, you can see the tips of the reeds swaying as some softly moving fish, perhaps of great size, makes its way through them. And when the light has gone you can hear rustlings and sucking noises, and an occasional great splash, which are somewhat alarming.' Later, in the same chapter, he says: 'In warm weather, carp swim near the surface and it does not take long to call their attention to floating bread.'

The first attempt Dick made resulted in a fish being hooked and breaking his line in short order. Remember, in those days Dick thought a size 8 hook was large and a 6lb line strong. His water, though, was heavily weeded and well featured with snags and lily pads. However, before the season had ended, he did get a fish of 9lb by 'margin fishing', which encouraged him to persist in it during the 1936 season which followed.

During that season, he learned that there was more in the method than just hanging a crust over the edge of the bank. Having the line taut would result in the carp sucking the crust clean off the hook, so Dick found it essential to have a foot or more of slack line between butt ring and reel. By 1936 Dick could boast quite a few carp caught by margin fishing, including some to what was then a fair size, 12lb 8oz.

The following year began with him feeling confident in the technique which had, by then, become so effective that he explained it to some friends. This confidence was not misplaced, for 1937 saw his first fifteen pounder. Other big fish were caught in the two seasons that followed, then came the war and with it little opportunity to fish, but in 1946 he was back after them again, and caught a fifteen and sixteen pounder in that year.

It was in that fateful year, 1946, that Dick was given a copy of 'B.B.'s' 'Fisherman's Bedside Book' and was so interested in what the author had to say about carp that he wrote to him. This letter appears in 'Confessions of a Carp Fisher'. B.B. came to stay with Dick Walker in 1947 and, in a week, landed five specimen carp by margin fishing.

Later, Dick explained the idea to Bernard Venables, who featured it in his 'Mr. Crabtree' fishing strip.

After this, things went from strength to strength and the 1951 season saw the first twenty pounder caught on such methods. In fact, looking at the records, several were caught that year, not only by 'margin fishing' but with the greater acceptance of floating crust as a method to use. One or two big carp had been captured by people just slinging out crust and finding a large carp had snaffled it up!

Throughout the fifties, the floating bait method gained more popularity as carp fishing became a more practised art. Its catching potential stretched across the complete spectrum of differing waters.

The Carp Catchers Club, that powerful band of specialist anglers (the original Specimen Group), heavily publicised the fact that carp were strong surface feeders and, in particular, could be caught after dark in the margins. Remember, 'night fishing' was very little practised by any fishermen at this time. In fact, when Richard Walker started telling anglers in the early fifties, through his weekly 'Angling Times' column, that he fished at night - and that the 'record 44lb carp' was caught in darkness - it prompted a hail of abuse. It was 'not fair' on the fish and it was deemed unsportsmanlike by someone, because the fishes' defences were down. Anyway, what fisherman alive would think of actively pursuing their quarry after dark - night time was for sleeping, everybody knew that - everybody except people like Richard Walker.

This lobby became so strong that voices went to the authorities asking for 'night fishing' to be banned. These misinformed souls thought people like Walker were cheating by fishing at night and that to catch a big carp at night was an easy affair!

I have here in the 'Carproom' cuttings from the popular press of the period and you would never believe the storm of controversy that raged at the time. Even Members of Parliament were lobbied to ban fishing at night. I'm glad to say, commonsense prevailed in the end, but for a while it was a close run thing.

I guess the outstanding success of the 'Carp Catchers' Club' started to rub off onto other anglers keen to adopt their methods. Richard Walker, for one, started to catch fish the like of which had never before been dreamed of; many of these were caught during darkness and for carp fishing he invented a device that helped detect a bite at night, the Electric Bite Alarm. Can you imagine the uproar this invaluable little device caused when the 'anti night fishing brigade', already feeling deflated once, found out about this contraption that 'electrocuted' fish!

We can laugh now about such extraordinary behaviour, but tempers were running high and, in all fairness, envy at what Richard Walker and friends were catching was at the heart of all these problems.

Trouble was, you would find it hard to argue with Walker, as his solid foundation of understanding fish's habits and the new way he looked at almost all aspects of freshwater fishing made him into a fishing Great. He banged the drum as far as surface fishing for carp was concerned, and the immediate effect he had on close friends was apparent. Maurice Ingham, that master carper from Lincolnshire and Carp Catchers' Club member, used this method when he first fished 'The Old Copper Mine', a water in Somerset. His catch on floating crust was important, as it showed the method worked on yet another water. I think it was the first time that Maurice had used the method and he wrote to Dick Walker in an enthusiastically worded letter. Bernard Venables (Mr. Crabtree), also used the method for the first time during this same period. His verdict - "a creditable carp catching method".

Carp Catchers Club member Maurice Ingham used the margin crust method when he fished the Old Copper Mine (Beechmere).

In the mid 1950's, Dick Walker proved beyond doubt that carp could be caught by margin fishing by providing photographic evidence in one of his weekly Angling Times columns. Though catching carp by this method had been done before, it had never been photographed, so Pete Thomas, Pat Russell and Dick thought they would try to get some pictures for Angling Times readers. Pete did the fishing, Dick worked the camera and Pat stood by with a supply of flash bulbs and a powerful torch. It proved a difficult business because an approaching fish was hard to see and it was exceedingly difficult to choose the right moment to shoot. After the flash had gone off, everyone was temporarily blinded, which did not make the proceedings either easy or safe, especially as Dick was perched upon a small platform jutting out into the lake with 7 feet of water only inches away. Margin fishing is an exciting business for the angler, but Dick concluded that it was even more exciting for a photographer!

Pete caught a 16lb carp for the camera and the pictures proved it. Best of all, Dick managed to photograph a carp that arrived unexpectedly. It broke surface in an attempt to reach a crust that was lifted several inches clear above the water, because small rudd had been worrying it. This picture alone gave evidence to the potential carp fishing public that carp were more than keen to get their lips around a bait, even when it was not in the water!

Dick's advice to the would be surface angler was as follows:

"Usually, small fish like rudd and roach will attack the crust and soon break it up. To prevent this, wind up the crust until it is a few inches above the water's surface and drop in a loose crust for the small fish to knock about. Their activities will attract carp and when one comes along, the small fish depart rapidly. You then lower the crust on your hook so that it floats but no line touches the water.

Keep a foot or so of slack between butt ring and reel and release this when the carp takes the bait so as to let him get his head down before you strike, otherwise you'll probably pull the hook out of his mouth. When you hit your fish, look out! He will turn like lightning and go out into the lake at a terrific pace and if your tackle can't pay out freely, you'll be smashed up instantly. While waiting for a carp to turn up, dip the hook bait in the water at intervals to keep it wet and soft. It can dry and harden quickly. Keep still and very alert and, having commenced fishing, don't move to another place. The carp will find your bait, given time. They seem nearly always to patrol in a clockwise direction, which means they will usually approach from your right. No, I don't know why!

Not only carp, but rudd, roach and tench also fall to margin fishing tactics on warm nights; of course, for these fish you must use smaller crusts, though a five pound tench can take a crust the size of a matchbox without any trouble.

Remember, the more heavily a water is fished in daylight, the better your chances with margin fishing after dark."

By now floater fishing was well and truly a standard part of a carp fisherman's tactics, although it was given a back seat. You will see reference to its uses in all the books on carp catching at the time. Towards the end of the fifties, this method made the headlines with a truly huge fish that had been captured from a lake in, of all places, a caravan park! Little was known about this venue in Berkshire as a carp fishery at the time, though we now know that it had indeed some good fish in it from way back.

In June 1959, a chap named Mr. J. Ward, who had tried in vain to capture some of the large carp which lived in this pond, was rewarded with a fish that was headline news. On the evening of 28th June, he tackled up with a humble bamboo rod and Intrepid fixed spool reel. The floating crust was cast near a dense weed bed where big carp were often seen lurking. Soon he hooked a big fish which refused to be beaten for over twenty minutes. Even then, if it had not been for a companion angler with a large landing net, we might not have seen the fish on the bank. Once landed, they found that no weighing scales were available to weigh a beast such as this, so the fish was hurried to Wokingham Railway Station where, in the Goods Office, it was calculated to weigh 34lb 8oz. The fish was then safely returned to the water. This, I think, was the first fully authenticated thirty pounder caught off the surface.

And so it has gone on. Redmire's first surface caught twenty pounder came in the early sixties, a carp of 26lb caught by one of the Taylor brothers. Fish were being reported from venues as different as large gravel pits to tiny, private estate lakes. The experiment in the bait itself, namely bread crust, went no further all through this period, although as we come to the end of the sixties, marshmallows - yes, marshmallows! - were being used with some success. Being different made all the difference, so to speak.

I think I'd better tell you about my introduction to the delights of floating crust. When I was very young (even I was young once), in the late fifties, I fished a local pond close to where I lived. In fact, when I say local, it was 365 paces from the back garden fence of my home to the bank of this pond. Interestingly, it is still a carp fishery today and, if you are wondering where it is, I'll tell you - Brittons Pond, near Guildford in Surrey. This magical place (as it seemed to us boys), had held carp from before the last war. They were of the long, almost 'wild' looking sort, common carp. There were a few of the mirror types there as well. To us kids who caught the gudgeon, small perch and the ever so occasional crucian carp, these larger carp were the fish of dreams, something that was impossible to hook, never mind land. We never caught one of these elusive monsters, not even by accident. Fishing with worms and bread paste, we were happy enough to see our float bob, go under and feel the thrill as another small wriggling perch came ashore. I can remember seeing those carp jumping and hearing them crash out of the water at night; they seemed to be beyond anything I could do, or even imagine I could do, to catch them. But what the heck, after dark there were other things to chase - girls!

Some time in the late fifties, there came to this pond to fish, men from London. They arrived just as the sun would be setting and stopped out all night. It was only then that I saw on the bank, at last, a **carp**. During the summer 'they' were successful in catching many of 'our' carp, but how? It must be because they fished through the night, we thought, but stopping out late and forgetting about the girls for once, made no difference to our catches. Before long though, the secret got out; they were using 'floating crust' straight on the hook; no float, no split shot, just the hook and a piece of crust off a loaf of bread!

I guess that was the first carp I ever caught - one on floating crust. It's more than thirty years ago now and, as you will by now have realised, I am still far from cured! With the undoing of those Brittons Pond carp with floating bread, it marked the start of my pursuit of carp that lasts to this day.

I also remember another water a bit further away, where a friend had gained permission for us to fish. It was one of those crazy places where the carp were half starved and, as I remember, only carp were present. Here it was amazing; throw out half a loaf when you arrived and within a minute the water would boil! Generally the carp were small, 2-6lb, but there were better fish there. The way to catch them was good old 'margin fishing'. You used to have to crawl along through the bamboo bushes right to the water's edge. Once there, flick out a few pieces to land right under your feet, in the edge. After a short while, better fish would show in the edge; when a bigger than average fish took a free piece, you would lower the hook bait and, bingo, you were away! One of the very first double figure carp I caught came like this and I've been hooked ever since!

The next step forward in bait came with the advent of the floater cake, generally made from the high protein ingredients that had started to revolutionise the catching of carp on the bottom. You simply added more eggs to the mix and baked, rather than boiled, the resulting mixture; it could then be cut into cubes, or any shape you liked. Adding a flavour came after this, as did colouring the bait.

Bait itself was not the only contributing factor to the increase of carp captures at this time. Long range fishing, with the bait coming up directly from a heavy lead, made quite an impact. Jack Hilton, a carp angler of some note, used long range crust fishing on waters in Kent and accounted for some tremendous catches in the sixties from what were then classified as hard waters. The particle approach of the pre-formed pet foods such as Chum, is something that has been with us for only a comparatively short time.

We have come a long way since H. T. Sheringham's advice, written in the

Floater country! Andy Little playing a fish on the sort of water that responds to observation, stalking and floaters.

early part of this century, to where floater fishing is today. The surface style of catching carp has proved, beyond doubt, that it can account for the downfall of even the largest carp that live in our waters. It's a fact, there have been carp over 40lb in weight captured off the top in this country, and all is set to stay this way, hopefully for many years to come.

As more people try their hand at this exciting form of carp fishing, the more the methods will become refined. This, along with improvements in bait and tactics, will, without doubt, make matters even better for the floater fisherman. Already I have seen an upsurge in enthusiasm in the last few years - I can only wish you luck from now on. Good fishing.

BAIT UP-DATE
Brian Skoyles

For the bulk of my surface fishing, the baits I would use fall into three categories:

(a)   Bottom base mixes made to float in some way.

(b)   Floater cakes.

(c)   Floating particles.

It is not uncommon for me to combine these in some way (loose feed particles but fish a piece of cake on the hook for example). All three have advantages and disadvantages. The best approach is probably to be aware of the possibilities that each bait has to offer and use that which is most appropriate on the day.

Looking at each one in detail:

(a) BOTTOM BASE MIXES MADE TO FLOAT IN SOME WAY

If you have a bait that is working well on the bottom, it can be very effective to just make that bait float. This makes the assumption that the carp are already accepting your bait so they will continue to do so when it is on the top. You can make bottom baits float in several different ways:

(1) **Inserts**. Most buoyant materials can be used as inserts for your baits; cork, polystyrene and foam are just three examples and they all work well. The principle is just to take a small square of material, which you think is the right size, mould some of your normal base mix around it and boil in the normal way. Let it cool off and test it in a cup etc. It it is nice and buoyant, cut some more pieces of material to the same size and make as many baits as you wish. It may take a little while to find the correct size of buoyant material, but once you have, you can make floating baits whenever you wish. The advantage of this system is that you end up with floating baits that are identical in size, smell and texture to your already established bottom bait. The disadvantage is that it can be very time consuming and fiddly to make and these baits can only be used as hook baits. Don't loose feed baits with polystyrene or cork inserts for obvious reasons. If you require free offerings use one of the alternative methods.

(2) **Baked or grilled**. Many base mixes can be made to float by baking or grilling. Times and temperatures will vary, depending on the ingredients in your base mix, so the following is a general approach, rather than a hard and fast sequence. Firstly, produce your usual base mix in the normal way. Line your grill pan or baking tray with baking foil (I'm not sure this has much effect on the finished baits, but it usually reduces the nagging in the background dramatically). Roll your base mix to the required size, set grill or oven to medium heat. Take half a dozen baits and cook for one minute; agitate the tray a bit so the baits cook evenly, take them out and allow to cool. Test in a cup and adjust the cooking time or temperature, or both, accordingly. I must admit, I'm not a fan of this method. I find it rather hit and miss and when I've got it right I'm still not sure if I've made an effective bait. My experience is that for many base mixes, to achieve consistent floating qualities requires a fairly long cooking time, producing side effects, such as making the bait lose a great deal of its texture and making them far too hard. On the other hand, some people that I've spoken to, recommend them highly so I'll have to try it again and you can make your own mind up. The advantages are that it can be used to produce a bait that nuisance fish don't succeed with very often. The disadvantages are that it is time consuming to make in large quantities.

(3) **Microwaved**. I must admit I'm not really into microwaved baits for a fairly basic reason - I haven't got a microwave! However, as they are a popular way of making pop-ups and floating baits, I've asked a mate of mine, Dave McMillan, for his comments and he suggests the following:

(a) Make your baits as normal.
(b) Allow to cool.
(c) Microwave in batches of about 20 on a low power setting. He suggests you slightly grease the plate with olive oil as some baits become sticky during the cooking time.
(d) Timing is difficult, but start with one minute then take 2 or 3 out and test them in a cup of water. Adjust cooking time accordingly.

Microwaved baits can be made very hard and very buoyant, but Dave reckons they lose their flavour and attractiveness. Having said that, I know of other anglers who rate them very highly.

(4) **Frybees**. I'm going to go into detail here, because I really rate these for surface fishing. They're not that easy to make until you get used to them, but when you do, the results can be worth the extra effort.

Apart from the usual mixing gear etc., you will need a small saucepan and a metal sieve that will fit into it. If you're making large quantities, a chip pan and fine meshed inner pan will do fine. You'll also need about a litre of good quality cooking oil (I use Flora).

Mix your base mix in the normal way and roll baits to the size you require. The temperature of the oil is critical so I always finish rolling the baits before messing about with the oil. Anyhow, when you are ready, put the oil on to heat up and have a few baits ready. When you think the oil is hot enough, try one bait. It should fry normally as you would cook chips etc. If this is happening, remove the pan from the heat (I do this because I've found that the oil can quickly become too hot and baits burn and blacken very quickly). It's then a case of frying your baits in small batches.

I dry them out on a kitchen towel and freeze in the required numbers. This means I only need to have a fry up once in a while, rather than messing around every time I do a mix.

Cooking time will vary, depending on your base mix. I try to judge the oil temperature so that the cooking time is roughly the same as I would boil the mix for bottom baits. I always remove the baits from the oil as soon as I notice them starting to brown slightly.

Baits cooked in this way have a very tough outer shell, but remain soft in the middle. They give off a beautiful oily smell and a slight oil slick in the water, which the carp seem to like.

On one occasion, I watched a carp move about underneath a patch of about a hundred flavoured Chum mixers. In this patch of mixers were four frybees. The patch extended over an area of perhaps half a tennis court. This one carp over about half an hour, picked off three or four Chum mixers and the four frybees. This, on a heavily pressured surface water where carp are very wary of all surface baits and tend to take few chances.

So, we can make our normal bottom base mixes float in a variety of ways, but overall I would suggest that they are rather limited as our main baits for floater fishing, possibly because they all take a long time to prepare, therefore making large quantities is a bit of a non-starter.

(b) FLOATER CAKES.

I would not want to floater fish regularly without having a range of floater cakes available and ready in my freezer. In a way, they are a bit like frybees in that they can make the difference between a take or two or a blank. With a little experimenting, it's possible to make a whole range of floater cakes and once you've got the hang of it, they are very easy. Again, as with the frybees, I tend to make several at a time and freeze them in small batches.

Most normal bottom base mixes can be converted into cake mixes, the main difference being the ratio between dry mix and eggs. Whereas for bottom baits you usually aim for a stiff paste, for floater cakes you usually aim for a thick soup. Most of my mixes, when complete, will **just** pour of their own accord into the cake tin (consistency of thick soup).

Going through the process: again, I won't give specific times, temperatures etc., as it will vary according to the base mix ingredients. I will, however, at the end of this description, give specific details of my two all time favourite recipes for floater cakes, together with some very successful flavour/oil combinations.

First the process. Get the oven and the baking tray ready first. The oven wants to be set at a medium heat (325°-375° F; 160°-190° C; Gas Mark 3-4). Arrange the shelves so that you can place your tray in the middle area. The tray I use is 7 inches square and I line this with kitchen foil and grease thoroughly with a good quality oil. (I use Flora). This is not preheated at all, just left standing ready to take the mix when it is ready for cooking.

To make the mix. In a medium mixing bowl, beat 4 large eggs, plus any colour/flavour you require. Make sure you do this thoroughly but don't go over the top, or use a mixer, so that you beat in too much air. Gradually add your dry mix, stirring well to produce a smooth, thick soup (it should just pour out of the bowl). Pour the mix into the lined baking tray and allow it to level off and settle. (I like a depth of approximately ½ inch). Leave for about 10 minutes then cook for the required time to produce a sponge type cake. Times will normally vary from between 30 minutes to 1¼ hours, depending on the type of base mix used. If you are using a base mix of your own I suggest that the first time you set the oven timer for 30 minutes and then keep checking every 10 minutes after that until you think it is cooked.

When it's ready, take it out of the oven and leave to cool. Try to peel off the foil (I say try, as some mixes stick very firmly to the foil) and then freeze until required. If the foil won't peel off, it's not important, leave it on and then it can be cut off individual chunks as you use it.

My two favourite floater cakes are as follows:

(1) Base Mix.

2oz Casein
3oz Full fat Soya flour
1oz Sodium Caseinate
2oz Wholewheat flour
1oz Fructose
1oz Wheat Gluten
½oz Vitmin (from S.B.S.)
The above ingredients are mixed thoroughly and will make more than one cake.

4 size 3 eggs
Colour and flavour (I've always rated either 2mls of Geoff Kemp's Mellow Brandy or 2mls of his Strawberry).

Cook for 30 minutes at 375°F, 190°C or Gas Mark 5.

MAKING FLOATER CAKE

!. Weighing out dry mix.
2. Lining the tray with foil.
3. Oil the tray.
4. Break eggs into bowl and beat
   thoroughly.
5. Add colour if required
6. Add flavour or oil.
7. Mix well.

Continued on next page.

FLOATER CAKE
(continued)

8. Add dry mix.
9. Mix well then pour
*   into tray.*
10. Level off.
11. Cook.
12. The finished cake.

Allow to cool then use or
freeze for use later.

(2) For the last two seasons I have switched from the above to, if anything, an easier alternative, in that it uses a ready mixed base mix.

     4oz Hi-Nu-Val (Nutrabaits)
     4 size 3 eggs

     As before, add the colour and flavour to the beaten eggs, then add the 4oz of Hi-Nu-Val.
     Cooking time for this one is 1 hour at a temperature of 325°F; 170°C or Gas Mark 4.
     With the above mix I've used various oil/flavour combinations, with some excellent results. My favourite attractor combinations are given below:

(a) 1 drop Spanish Red Thyme Oil
     $^{1}/_{2}$ml Sweet Cajouser

(b) 2 drops Cassia Oil
     $^{1}/_{2}$ml Sweet Cajouser
     (both the oils and Sweet Cajouser can be obtained from Nutrabaits).

     In fairness to other suppliers, I'm not suggesting that the above are the only ones that will work well. I field test flavours and oils for Nutrabaits so I have personal experience of the above but, equally, friends have tried oils and flavours from other bait suppliers with very good results.

At this point it might also be worth mentioning how I present floater cake on the hook, as I have a favourite way of doing this.

Carp often swirl and test the larger types of floating baits before they are finally sucked in. I need a method of hooking a bait on that will not be affected by these initial swirls or sucks i.e. so that the position of the hook within the bait stays where I want it.

Straight hooking does not do this. It looks good to start with, as you put the fresh bait on but after casting and soaking up some water, the bait often slides to the bend of the hook, giving you rubbish presentation

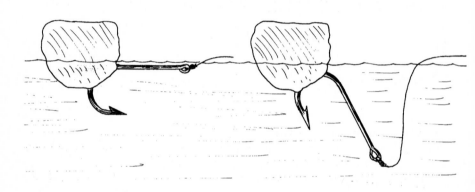

Diagram 1

Likewise, I am not too happy with hair rigs etc., for this type of fishing because the hook can be snagged on weed or, more importantly, foul hook fish as they investigate the bait.

The method described below solves these problems and although a little fiddly to tie, is very easy thereafter to use.

The principle is to use a small length of pole elastic, slightly shorter than the thickness of the floater cake, that is held in position by a piece of tight rig tubing to the shank of the hook.

Hopefully, the diagram will make it easy to understand.

If you use a hook with a straight eye and a wide gape (the Partridge 22's are perfect for this) and cut a small notch in the rig tube, the whole lot will stay in place, no matter how hard you cast, or how many times the fish inspects the bait.

Diagram 2

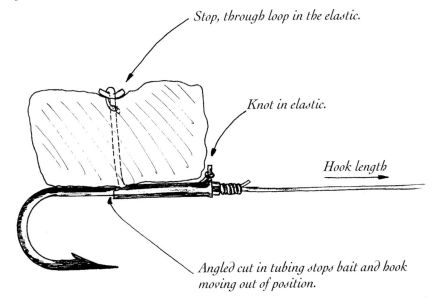

Stop, through loop in the elastic.

Knot in elastic.

Hook length

Angled cut in tubing stops bait and hook moving out of position.

(c) FLOATING PARTICLES

For the last few years this has been the big one. Literally thousands of carp have been caught on a wide variety of floating particles.

As with any other bait type, some floating particles are better than others. For that reason I'll mention many, but concentrate on those that have proved to be the most consistent. With a bit of luck this will point you in the right direction and you might find some others of your own that are equally effective.

A floating particle is, basically, any food source that can be obtained in (or cut up into) small pieces that float. This covers a wide spectrum, and includes various seeds, breakfast cereals, children's snacks, cat foods, dog foods and various fish/animal pellets, either used as they come or treated in some way.

Of these, I rate the cat and dog foods as by far the best. The seeds (sunflower is the classic example) have caught carp, but take a long time to become established and, in my case, on several lakes were completely ignored. Having said that, other people rate them, so it's up to you. The cereals and children's snacks are definitely liked by the carp, but present all sorts of problems when it comes to using them.

First of all, they are very light and almost impossible to catapult into the water. In any sort of wind, particularly facing you, they'll drive you round the bend, often ending up behind you. The fish like them if you can get them into the water. I've had fish going mad over Sugar Puffs and Start in particular, but then comes problem number two. All these cereals are designed to soak up milk, so they often soak up water. This means that you have a problem in using them as a hookbait as, basically, no matter what you do, they often soften and break up far too quickly.

Of the snacks, pop corn and Hoola-hoops are probably the best but, again, they are very light and can be difficult to use. Talking about children's snacks has reminded me about another great floater bait from years gone by - marshmallows. Carp love them and if it starts to rain, or there are no fish on top, you can always eat them!

Back to particles. I would suggest that the best advice at this stage is 'keep an open mind'. I make a point of dropping one of any snack that comes out, into a cup of water. Mind you, it does upset the kids at times when I nick their goodies.

The same advice could be given for cat and dog biscuits, there are many to choose from. Most make excellent floater baits; my favourites being Brekkies, Go-Cat, Pedigree Chum Mixers (more about them later), Choosy and Meow Mix.

If you are fishing for very experienced fish, two more to add to that list are Small Bite Mixers and Delicat. These two mini-particles can be superb if you can fish close in. Delicat is particularly useful as it comes as a softish biscuit in sealed foil sachets, which means you can always leave a few sachets in the car in case you come across fish when you are not particularly expecting them to be on top (middle of winter, for example).

Most of these cat and dog biscuits are hard to start with, so you have a decision to make. Are you going to use them hard, or are you going to soften them first? There are advantages and disadvantages either way.

Used Hard

Advantages: Ready to use quickly. Immune to small fish for longer.

Disadvantages: My personal feeling is that carp are not quite so attracted to harder baits, or perhaps they don't eat quite so many, as they tend to swell up a little as they soften and so, perhaps, 'fill the carp up'. Harder to use as hookbait. Need to be glued or tied on (takes longer).

Used Soft

Advantages: Easy to put on the hook etc. I think they tend to smell more.

Disadvantages: Don't last so long in the water. Must be prepared in advance, often the day before. Once softened, they will start to go off if not frozen after a session.

On balance, I prefer to soften the baits I use, but I know of many anglers who use these types of bait straight from the box or packet and do very well. As with most things in angling, it's for you to think about and try. Generally it's a case of what you have most confidence in.

If I just want to soften a particular brand of dog or cat biscuit, I use the following method.

Start off by half filling a plastic box with dry biscuits. Any box will do, as long as it has a secure lid. (The half litre margarine tubs are ideal for this).

Pour hot water over the biscuits, snap on the lid, slightly open one corner and quickly drain off the hot water. Snap the lid shut and shake the container vigorously for several minutes (at least until the biscuits stop steaming). If you don't do this stage properly, the biscuits will stick together.

Leave to cool completely; shake again to make sure the biscuits are not stuck together, then transfer to a plastic bag and leave overnight.

One advantage of this method is that you can add extra flavours etc., to the water before you pour it over the biscuits, therefore giving you the chance to personalise a particular bait.

One bait, above all others, can be treated with different flavours and colours. I refer to Pedigree Chum Mixers. This is a good bait, as it can either be used hard, or softened by the above method. Adding a colour or a flavour can make them sensational.

If you want to add a colour/flavour combination to mixers, you could use the method already described for softening biscuits, but it has one major disadvantage, that is, you quickly pour off the water and therefore a lot of the colour/flavour goes down the sink and not into the bait. For this reason, I use a different method for flavouring mixers.

You will need a large, good quality freezer bag and a small drinks bottle with 160mls of water in it. (I use a small pop bottle with some tape round it at the 160mls level). This means I can soften and flavour baits at the waterside without having to much about measuring 160mls each time.

The method: Put 1½lb of dry mixers in the freezer bag. Add any powdered colour you wish at this stage and shake the bag so that the colour is evenly spread. To the 160mls in the pop bottle, add any flavour you wish. Screw the top on securely and shake well.

Have a bag-tie ready. Pour the liquid into the freezer bag; gather the top of the bag together, blow into it and then seal it very tightly so you have a large freezer bag balloon. Shake thoroughly. At first the colour and flavour will colour the bag completely and the baits will stick together. Keep shaking and after 5 minutes or so, the baits will start to soak up the water, being flavoured and coloured at the same time. You will know when to stop because the bag will go completely clear. Leave overnight. In the morning the baits can be transferred to another bag and put in the freezer where they will keep for months.

I normally have several bags ready for use in the freezer. When I go fishing I normally take them in a cool box, then any I don't use can be put back in the freezer; even those that have thawed out can still be refrozen without any apparent ill effect on their attractiveness.

My favourite colours are, without doubt, brown, red or orange. I'm not sure this has much effect on the fish as I think most appear very dark from underneath anyhow, but they do seem to be the best compromise between ultimately beaten him to the floater.

COLOURING /FLAVOURING MIXES

1. *Measure out quantity. (One and a half pounds to 160 mils of water).*
2. *Add flavour to water.*
3. *Pour flavoured water into bag.*
4. *Blow in the bag then seal.*
5. *Shake thoroughly for at least five minutes then leave overnight. Freeze if necessary.*

visibility for fishing and not attracting wildfowl from more than 50 yards (sometimes). Flavours are up to you. As with the floater cake, I've been using some Nutrabaits gear for the last two years and the following are my favourites.

All are quoted for a 1½lb weight of mixers.

(1) 2ml Sweet Cajouser
     2ml Crafty Catcher Peanut

(3) 3 drops Spanish Red Thyme
     1ml Sweet Cajouser

(2) 6 drops Cassia
     1ml Sweet Cajouser

(4) 2ml Strawberry Nutrafruit
     2ml Cherry Nutrafruit

The above have all caught very well for me but as I've already said, many other flavours/oils etc., sold by other companies will also do well.

As with floater cake, it is important how you put the bait on the hook. For single particle floaters I use two methods:

(a) The Easy Method for Easy Fish.

This requires an eyed hook and you need to be able to tie the grinner knot (Diagram 3).

DIAGRAM 3

Stages in tying the knot.

1. Thread line through eye and fold it around the main line four times.

2. Take the loose end and thread it through the loop nearest the hook eye, leave a largish loop.

3. Fold the loose end through the loop 4 times and then pull the loose end along the line of the mainline. This will close up the knot leaving it some way up the main line.

4. Wet the line and slide the knot down to the hook eye.

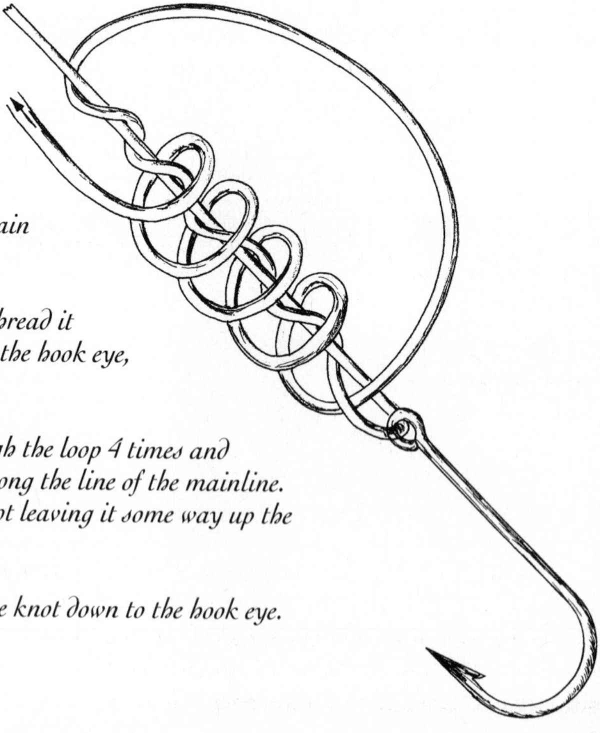

The idea is that the grinner knot, when tightened, has its spare line coming out of the top of the knot, pointing back up the main line. If this is cut off, leaving ¼ inch or so sticking out, it serves as a catch for the bait, so that the bait does not slide back to the bend of the hook.

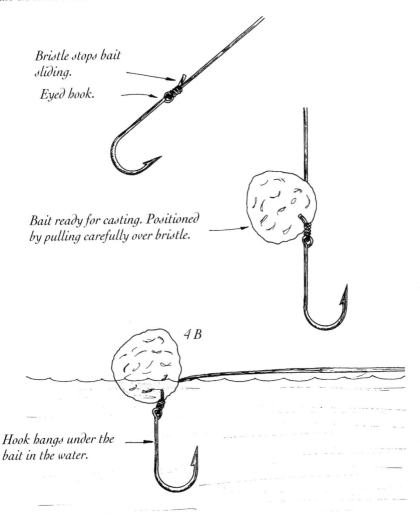

Bristle stops bait sliding.

Eyed hook.

Bait ready for casting. Positioned by pulling carefully over bristle.

4 B

Hook hangs under the bait in the water.

I'm happy with this easy way of hooking the bait as it means the hook always ends up underneath the bait in the ideal spot to hook the fish.

If the bait slips on to the bend of the hook however, the reverse is true and the eye of the hook sinks, putting the hook in the worst position. This method only works, of course, for softened baits.

(b) The Adjustable Hair.

A slightly more reliable method that can also be used for hard baits, is to use a small hair trapped in place with two very small, but tight, pieces of rig tubing. This idea was originally sent to me by Mike Kavanagh (Carp Society Chairman) for use in the Top Tips Section of the Society magazine. I did use it there and I've since used it to catch many carp. It is described in Diagram 5.

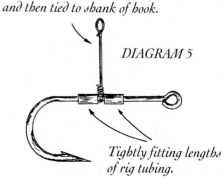

Appropriate length of line looped at one end and then tied to shank of hook.

DIAGRAM 5

The idea is, you tie on a small hair and trap it in place with the two pieces or rig tubing. Once you've done this, lower it in the water with a bait held on the hair with a boilie stop of small V of grass stem etc. You can then move the two pieces of tubing up and down the shank of the hook until the hook is perfectly balanced underneath the bait. (Diagrams 6a, 6b and 6c).

Tightly fitting lengths of rig tubing.

Hard baits can be used on this set up by quickly drilling them out with a nut drill first, or soft baits can be put on using a standard fine point boilie needle.

Another method that can also be used is a scaled down version of the method already described for floater cake (Diagram 2), although if you do, it is important not to put too much tension on the pole elastic as it can pull out of the particle as the bait softens.

DIAGRAM 6

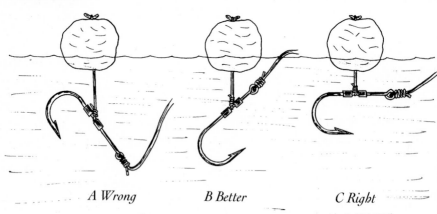

A Wrong   *B Better*   *C Right*

Double baits are also very effective and it can pay to experiment, trying first a single hookbait and then a double on the next cast. Some days they seem to prefer one, another day a double. Why? I don't know.

If I am using a double, I usually use a double looped hair positioned on the shank of the hook with a small piece of tight rig tubing. (Diagram 7).

DIAGRAM 7

Again, I try this rig out in the margins to make sure the hook is balanced.

If you want to put the hook a little lower in the water when using a double bait, another method is to use the double looped hair but trap it between the eye of the hook and the knot before you pull the hooklength knot tight (Diagram 8).

DIAGRAM 8

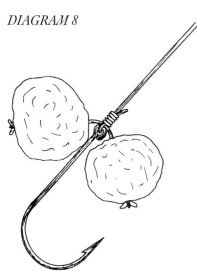

I prefer this version if I'm casting hard, as it cannot slip and seems to be reasonably tangle proof.

So there is a very good range of floating particles. If you don't fancy the cat and dog biscuits, there are several types of fish pellets that float and they can be brilliant. It's up to you; be open-minded and be prepared to experiment. Remember, the one big advantage that the floater angler has, is that he can watch the fish's reaction to what you are doing.

Having said that, don't be too impatient. I'm normally not too worried if I drift a new bait over fish and they ignore it first off. If I try it over several sessions and nothing happens, I might think again but it could be that they need a while to get used to the idea that whatever you are trying is a nice new food for them.

Sometimes you'll get it wrong, but believe me, if you persevere and eventually get it right, you'll be in for some spectacular fishing.

TACKLE AND TECHNIQUE
Chris Ball

Outlined here is the tackle I use, and have done so for some time now, for floater fishing.

RODS.

My favourite rod is over 10 years old; it's a rod which Alan Brown Developments used to put out under the name of the Rod Hutchinson 'Seeker'. It's 9ft and built of fibreglass; has a test curve of 1½lb and is strong, yet forgiving in action. I've yet to find a replacement in amongst the Carbon/ Kevlar works of art that have been produced in these last 10 years. It's got a Fuji clip reel-fitting that keeps the reel well and truly in position, in fact, I haven't taken the reel off the rod for quite a few seasons now. This firm reel fixture is important, as the pressure and strain that is sometimes exerted on this little rod means it's vital for the reel to stay firm.

This rod gets dragged through bushes, tree branches and generally gets abused, yet surprisingly, needs little in the way of maintenance. It is an incredible fishing rod - because it's equally at home fishing under the rod tip in heavy snags with 15lb line as it is fishing at range with just 6lb line; I find it perfect.

However, the only time I try a variation is in a situation of open water fishing with no snags present. Here I would use a **Split Cane Rod.** Yes! I did say a Cane Rod. They are lovely to play fish on and bring back a nice piece of nostalgia when I am out and about. Don't for one minute think they are floppy and fragile - the ones I use have mastered many a carp that are at their ideal fighting weight, around 15-18lb. Of the several that I use, just two stand out.

The first is a **J. B. Walker Mk. 1V Avon.** These rods you could buy from the early 1950's onwards, but only in kit form. You had the cane supplied ready built with the metal ferrules already in position; you then had to complete the rest, i.e. fix and shape the cork handle, then whip the rings on and finally, varnish off. This actual rod I rebuilt myself five years ago, for it was in a sorry state when first acquired. The cane was fine, by that I mean it was not damaged, nor had it taken a **set** of any sort. The cane was typical of what J. B. Walker produced in the fifties and was first class. With quite hard abuse, it comes through with flying colours. This rod is a super little weapon to use where I would expect carp to be no bigger than 20lb.

For heavier fish, again in clear water, or at best, a lightly weeded water, then I would go for a '**Bob Southall' built cane Mk. 1V Carp Rod.** This has a test curve of 1½lb and has a classic 'compound taper' Mk. 1V carp rod action the like of which that late, great angler, Richard Walker devised. Again, I undertook to completely refurbish it. It dates from the late 1950's and represents the ultimate in split cane construction. 'Bob Southall' hand-made cane rods (especially the carp rods) are much sought after these days amongst tackle collectors. I count myself lucky enough to own **two** of his Mk. 1V's. Even some of the mighty Savay carp have, in recent times, fallen to this rod - that was before the weed became too bad - for I landed several on the 'Southall'. It is an incredibly strong rod that is a joy to use and, besides the nostalgia bit, it's efficient in subduing big carp in the conditions I have described.

REELS.

On to reels. Again, it's personal preference and these days the range seems endless. My own reels are a mixture of old, well worn favourites that display the most important aspect that any item of tackle needs - that is, solid reliability.

The number one reel I have used for the last 30 years (same one!) is the **Mitchell 301** (the 301 is the left hand version of the time honoured standard 300 Mitchell). It has never let me down and I don't think it ever will, so I have no real need to change but, as variety is the spice of life, I do use others from time to time.

Again it's the vintage fixed spool reels that I go for. The **'Ambidex Reel'** may not be a name you are aware of these days: although manufacturing ceased some time ago, their durability means you will find many still in circulation. I have a few different models: all of them run like silk and have a good, sensitive clutch assembly.

Always carry spare spools with you. A good range would be 6lb, 8lb, 10lb and 15lb. This will cover most needs and see you through a varied day's fishing. One luxury you will find indispensable is to carry two rods set up, one with light line and a heavy controller on, the second set up with the 10lb or 15lb line.

To get the most out of floater fishing and be really successful, you must be adaptable and make the most of any opportunity that appears. Using just one rod can be a pain, as during the course of just a few hours' fishing, you could encounter both extremes of either long range, light line fishing, or heavy lily pond stalking. You will notice these comments are all biased towards a truly mobile approach as in my own floater style: no lazing on bedchairs I'm afraid!

LINES.

On to recommended lines for surface fishing. For many years I used **Maxima** or **Platil**, but not **Sylcast**. I always found that it retained its 'spool memory' and left ugly coils on the surface (until I hooked a fish). All lines do this of course, to a greater or lesser extent.

The best all round line was Maxima and this has served me well for 15 odd years now. In 6lb breaking strain for open water fishing, it is superb and, coupled with the little 9ft stalking rod which I have mentioned, I have landed literally hundreds of carp on it. Only on a few occasions have I run into trouble and lost a fish that got caught in some bankside snags. The reason why this particular combination is so good is that it's perfectly balanced; it's difficult to break the line - honest! Using an unsuitable rod will lose you fish after fish.

In the main, during recent years I've used a hook link of the same breaking strain as the main line, normally making the hooklink up with a swivel which is used as a stop that the controller will rest against. In snag fishing at close range, just tie the hook straight onto the line. You don't need a casting weight on the line.

Now, in this style of fishing I would always use **'Sylcast'** or **'Brent'** because I feel it's tougher when any kind of snag is present. These views will be echoed by most experienced carp men, but times change and technology moves forward. In fishing line the revolution is in producing a thinner line, but still of a high breaking strain.

Years ago, 0.25mm line would have been rated as 6-8lb breaking strain, but now, coming onto the market are lines which offer 10-12lb breaking strain but with no increase in line thickness. They are generally pretty good but you must remember that they are still susceptible to damage as a 0.25mm thickness line, not the standard as thicker 10 or 12lb line. Hope that makes sense - I know what I mean!

My recent experiences suggest that there is some mileage in these hi-tech products. One that I can recommend is the **D.A.M. Spezi-line**. In 0.25mm this gives a knot strength over 11lb. All this means is that you have the characteristics of ordinary 6lb line, but the increased confidence and greater margin for error of 11lb breaking strain. This particular line also exhibits a very shiny surface so there's no need to heavily grease it.

LANDING NETS.

Amongst other items you will need in a stalking approach to floater fishing is your landing net. Again, this is an area which I have looked at seriously, having gone through many landing nets over the years. For the last five years I have used a special net made by my friend Steve Neville. It's different to most nets available in so much as the arms are heavily bowed. The arms are 36" but the throat of the net (the front) is just 28" wide. This is very useful for poking into small gaps and the like. One place I fish, under some rhododendrons, where the fishing is tight to say the least, it has proved itself time after time. The whole net is made from fibreglass and is very durable. The handle is tapered with a dural point fitted at the end. Again, it's very useful to have the net stuck in the ground, the water, or soft mud if you are hidden in amongst reeds because the net is easy to get at – and light because the net itself is kept dry until you use it. The practice of placing the net in the water every time you stop at a likely looking spot is largely a waste of time and makes the net always heavy to carry. You won't mind this if you've landed a fish, but it's annoying when you are searching for fish and carrying it wet.

The net itself, or should I say the material, is, I feel, important. The soft green micro-mesh ones are the ones to look for. Again, I'm not too keen on the dual mesh nets; they are heavier and often over large. Look for a depth of around 4ft deep.

Bait Bag.

Although you can carry odd bits of tackle in your pockets, a vital piece of equipment is a small tackle bag. The Kevin Nash 'Stalker' bag is fine and can contain just about everything you need for a day's fishing, but you can go lighter.

All you really need is a bag to hold your bait, small items of tackle and weigh slings, sacks and scales. These bags exist, but you need to look at trout fishing bags; the ones with the netting in the front. One of my mates started using his trout bag for floater fishing and found that it was ideal; the netting at the front can hold a wet sling and sack, thereby saving your tackle box and things from ending up wet. It's a good idea, so watch out for a Kevin Nash version (maybe).

The magic bag of tricks.

Polaroids.

Another important item is Polaroid glasses. Why all fishermen haven't got a pair is a mystery to me. Probably the best are the Optix Cormorants, but I use Boots' own brand at around £8-10. I have two sets, one with the grey lens, the other with the brown/bronze lens. Why two? Well, for dirty water, which is invariably sandy looking, I find the brown/bronze lens the best, whereas for gin clear gravel pit water the grey lens seems to be best.

Hat.

To further improve your vision, wear a peaked hat. Shielding the tops of the frames with the palms of your hands is okay, but not that satisfactory. When you shield the tops of glasses it makes a great deal of difference and I would advise anyone to wear some sort of peaked hat. The flat hats can make your head sweat like fury in hot weather, so try an American baseball type cap.

By using Polaroids and a peaked cap, you will start seeing fish which you would otherwise miss, especially in a heavy ripple.

2. HOW TO PRESENT A BAIT OUT ON THE WATER

It's surprising, but with only a couple of pieces of Chum on the hook you will find with light line you can cast quite a few yards, but really you need some sort of controller to add weight to your end rig.

Many years ago, these were unheard of, and when presenting a surface bait this was in the form of a ledger weight stopping some feet away from the bait so the line came up vertically from the lead to the bait.

In one of my local tackle shops I found, in the late seventies, a float called a 'BONNARD'. It came in several sizes (weights) but the last thing it was used for was carp fishing. A few of us started to use them as controllers. They were ideal and have served us very well during the years. The way to use them is quite simple, but here are a few modifications that will make life simpler.

Firstly, don't attach the controller directly to your line, there are two small holes at the top end of the 'Bonnard' which is coloured red. Enlarge the top hole with a small knife or one blade of your fishing scissors; make it about $1/6$th diameter. You can now attach a link swivel easily through this enlarged hole and fix to either a swivel or a swivel bead like the John Roberts type.

This can then take the main line through it and, as can be seen, it's free running on the line. This is not desirable, so you need some sort of stop behind the controller to fix it, something like a ledger stop or, better still, a rubber float stop. D.A.M. make the best sort; ask your tackle dealer.

With his set up you would have the hook link made up with a swivel on the end, for this provides a stop for the controller, coupled with the float stop

A selection of controllers - and a very successful bait.

behind it, you have effectively fixed the controller on the line. Why is the link swivel set-up used? Well, by putting the line through one of the small holes in the 'Bonnard' means if you want to change to a heavier or lighter controller, and sometimes you will want to do this quickly, you have to break the tackle down. With the link swivel method, you can change easily and quickly to any size you like without touching the line or end rig.

Tangling can occur sometimes because the light bait gets dragged behind the controller, especially when you cast heavily. You can get round this with a piece of rig tube with a 'John Roberts' link ledger bead attached, about a $2\frac{1}{6}$" length is about right. Then attach the controller with the link swivel and you will have a first class general purpose set-up, one that will be efficient in most circumstances.

As well as the 'Bonnard', there are now many other versions of controllers; all of them sit up in the water vertically with a varying amount of the top showing. Some of the best are the ones produced by Kevin Nash and Terry Eustace; they come in various sizes and are well made. In the casting stakes the Terry Eustace 'floater floats' are excellent and are tangle free. Again, lock them tight onto the line so that, in effect, they become bolt rigs.

There are several other ways to present your floating food, and these are the methods to use when your fish are becoming cute and spotting the line. Both methods rely on no line touching the water **anywhere** near the hook bait. Both are very effective and can fool fish for some considerable time.

The first is the **'Gardner Suspender'**. This is an ingenious device that few people bother to use. It works on the principle of a stem made out of strong tubing about 1ft in length. At one end is a weight in the form of a circular tube of metal about $1\frac{1}{2}$" long. Just above that is a large poly ball which is pierced through the centre and fixed to the stem. Your main line is threaded up through the stem, then you join it to a short hook link. The swivel of the hook link is jammed into a soft rubber sleeve at the end of the stem. When you attach a bait to the hook and drop the lot into the water, the stem cocks at a 45° angle, so the hook link goes down vertically with the bait and hook balanced perfectly so they just touch the water's surface. There is no line touching the surface in the immediate vicinity of the hook bait; although the stem and poly ball are close by, their presence seems not to arouse the carp's suspicions. It might sound ungainly, but it works surprisingly well.

Two tips:

1.   Grease the stem of the 'Suspender' as this makes it pop out of the water and not stick to the surface tension.

2.   Make sure the hook link is about 6" as this gives the right presentation and cocks the float correctly. This controller is also a bolt rig as the swivel of the hook link is semi fixed inside the rubber sleeve.

Besides the advantage of no line on the water near the bait, it also has an important plus in the fact that it freely drifts around and can be used in a ripple. I say this because the last method I'll mention is almost the ultimate in bait presentation because no line, not even the main line touches the water. It is a fixed method where the bait is cast out and stays in one position, which can be good or bad.

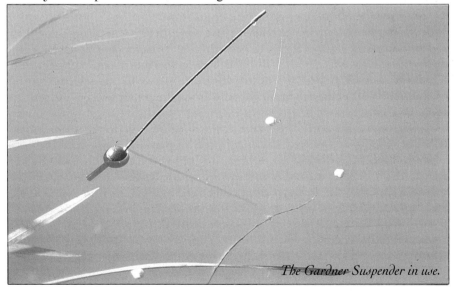

The Gardner Suspender in use.

This rig, of course, is the much publicised **Beachcaster Rig**. There is little doubt that even the most 'line spooky carp' can be caught on this rig and it can take some time before they wise up. This method entails the use of a heavy lead at the end of the line, then attach a pike bung or similar size float to fish just over depth. The hook link is tied in about 2ft above the bung from a three way swivel. Now the bait will sit on the surface with no line touching if the rod is propped up just off the vertical. There are special rod rests you can now buy for fishing the rod in this manner.

Make no mistake about it, it's one hell of a rig and one that you can relax when fishing, for the fish will hook themselves against the tension of the tight line/heavy lead. This is where a 'Baitrunner' style reel comes into its own, as you can finely tune the tension so the rig sits perfectly on the water and provides the necessary tautness so the carp is hooked in a flash.

The only minus I can see with it, is that it is in a fixed position out in the water. This might not, on the face of it, appear to be a problem, but if the rig is used by many on your water the carp will wise up to the fact that it's stationary, when the freebies are moving. You might find this hard to believe as it would appear that this presentation is perfect and the carp feel safe, but they **will** wise up to this. The problem becomes worse if, as often is the case, there is a ripple on the water. Saying all that, it's still very effective and it will be some time before the stage I've just outlined is reached.

No line touching the water is not new when one looks at surface fishing. The original method, employed by Richard Walker and friends, that of 'margin fishing', allowed the line to hang vertically down, straight off the rod end, which was poked out over the water. Don't ignore this method because it will work on many waters. For instance, if you are night fishing, try throwing out some surface free samples, then keep your eyes and ears open because the carp will often skirt the margins, especially after dark. Hardly anyone tries this approach these days - you could be surprised! It's likely to work on any water so long as there is sufficient depth of water in the margins. You can use whatever strength of line you like, because only the baited hook touches the water. It can be tremendously exciting fishing this way in the dark.

These kind of methods, i.e. 'slightly off the beaten track approach' can be rewarding and fool some big fish because they are different. The fish are rarely hooked in the margins anymore, let alone on the surface, that's why it appeals to me.

There is a good case to be made for this 'night stalking' with floating tactics; it's something you can think about once you've mastered (and been successful) at floater fishing in the daylight.

The drawings on pg 43 were prepared from originals supplied by Dave Miller and first appeared in Carp Fisher 20.

STANDARD BEACH CASTER RIG

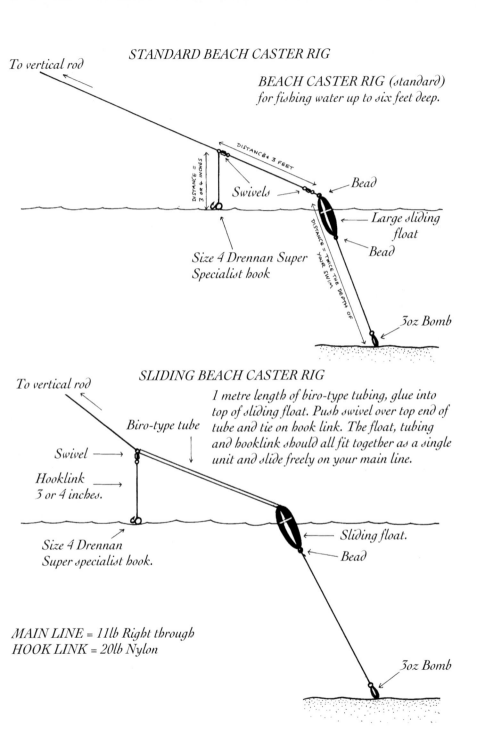

To vertical rod

BEACH CASTER RIG (standard)
for fishing water up to six feet deep.

DISTANCE = 3 FEET

DISTANCE = 3 OR 4 INCHES

Swivels

Bead

Size 4 Drennan Super
Specialist hook

Large sliding
float

DISTANCE = TWICE THE DEPTH OF YOUR SWIM

Bead

3oz Bomb

SLIDING BEACH CASTER RIG

To vertical rod

Biro-type tube

1 metre length of biro-type tubing, glue into
top of sliding float. Push swivel over top end of
tube and tie on hook link. The float, tubing
and hooklink should all fit together as a single
unit and slide freely on your main line.

Swivel

Hooklink
3 or 4 inches.

Size 4 Drennan
Super specialist hook.

Sliding float.

Bead

MAIN LINE = 11lb Right through
HOOK LINK = 20lb Nylon

3oz Bomb

3. RIGS.

There are many ways to present a surface bait: all of them have certain advantages and disadvantages. First, the most straightforward way is freelining, just a hook attached. The bait, say bread crust, can easily be attached to the hook by just piercing the crust with the hook point, then twisting it round to bring it back so the bend pulls down to sit on the 'crusty' side of the bread. Try a piece around $^3/_4$" square with about $^1/_2$" of flake showing. Don't worry if this looks big when compared to a piece of Chum mixer, look at the size of a carp's mouth! Even when dry, the bread will be heavy enough to flick out 5-19 yards, but you will find that a slight 'dunk' (or dip) into the water will help considerably. Be careful not to overdo this as the bread acts as a sponge and becomes flimsy, you can easily cast if off! The line that you cast out will float (or should) on the water's surface. This is floater fishing at its simplest and purest and it can still catch carp.

For instance, you might find a carp swimming close by some lily pads. Every now and then his mouth might investigate some item or other on the surface. If you don't frighten this fish and cast, ideally in line to where he is moving, there is every chance that he'll stop and investigate. If he does and remember, some won't, you stand a chance of hooking him. First time this happens, you will probably 'fluff' it, either strike too early, wait, or hesitate as he investigates this unexpected goodie. This is what I call 'sampling'. It happens so often that on some waters it represents a real problem when trying to hook fish. This is where rigs come into play, for there are ways round the hooking problem that are presented by a carp.

Let's look at the humble hook to start with. There are many good hooks around these days; these are some of the ones I suggest you look at.

A good 'open water' hook and one I've landed many carp on is the **'Drennan Specialist'**. This is one of the patterns that started the 'chemically sharpened' revolution that now has become almost the standard in this country for making a super sharp hook point. Used in small sizes (10 or 12), they are superb. I've landed fish to almost 25lb on a size 10! Surprisingly strong, they go in in a flash and stay in. People have, in the past, criticised these ultra sharp hooks, saying that they tear at the flesh and pop out. It's not my experience, in the main. The problem that presents itself is getting the darn things out, even though they have a small barb.

In the basic set-up of controller, 4ft hooklink and small hook, I would almost certainly make the hooklink float. Depending how pressurised your fish are, you will get chances on this presentation. The bites can vary from the most subtle detectable movement around the hook bait, which at range you won't spot, to a massive swirl like a depth charge going off. In between these two extremes, there can be dozens of variants, all of which include the fish 'sampling' the hook bait in some shape or form, trying to make sure if it's safe to eat. Sounds simple, but that's what they're trying to do.

In the main, the line is the biggest problem we have to get round. If you are faced with repeated swirls at the hookbait, the first ploy to try is to make the hooklink sink. This is simple, a spot of washing up liquid just rubbed between your fingers and applied to the line will make it sink. It works because no longer do we have the line silhouetted as it lies on the surface. This, without doubt, scares some fish; so much so that all your free samples are often mopped up but your hook bait is there in splendid isolation, not even being inspected. Sinking the hooklink can help, but you run the risk of the carp touching this sunken line just as he comes close to the hook bait. This again can cause problems as they become 'spooky' to this method, but it does work. The problem needs to be tackled from a different angle and I'll come to this later.

People often wonder how you attach a hard bait, such as Chum Mixer, to the hook. These pre-soaked dog and cat biscuits provide the surface angler with a terrific bait that is so convenient it's hard to change to anything else. You'll see how versatile these are as the story unfolds!

With any of these, the simplest way is to soak them, but only for a very short time, then leave in an air tight bag for a few hours. This means that you will be able to impale them easily onto the hook. Dependent on hook size, you will be able to use one or two pieces of Chum. This is still the 'standard' method of using Chum or almost any of the pre-shaped pet foods.

If your carp are feeding well and display what I call 'competitive feeding', you will be in with a good chance of hooking your fish, but as carp become more crafty or shy of the hook bait, they will carefully inspect **all** baits, not just the hook bait. This behaviour is what I mean by 'sampling'. It is here that mounting the bait on some kind of hair is an advantage. It works just as well on the surface as with a bottom bait, working on the principle of the hook being bare and hanging free.

For a long time, the most effective rig I found was to tie a loop of 1lb line round a piece of Chum and knot it firmly, say a double granny, then carefully thread the end of the hair line through the eye of the hook, again with a double granny knot. You will find that you can pull the free end of the hair and the line will come through the double granny so that it moves the Chum back towards the eye of the hook. You aim to get the Chum just touching the hook . This set up, when using a very sharp, small hook, will catch the carp out because of the hair rig set up.

Imagine the crafty old carp swimming around taking the odd free samples. He can maybe see our floating line in the vicinity and will be suspicious, but he is not the only carp present. Others around him may well be less cautious - different fish can be less suspicious, believe me, dependent on the amount of food present/amount of fish present. He will be looking carefully at each bait sample, often by extending the top lip over the bait so gently you would never believe. This is where presenting the bait on the hair wins, because it does not mask in any way the hook or hook point. Our carpy friend only has to touch the bait and feel danger (the line) and will try to eject, when bingo, the hook takes hold. The hook link straightens, then he feels the resistance of the fixed controller; by then you will have struck - hopefully! I cannot stress enough that you must concentrate on the hook bait at all times, where possible.

Floater fished off the back of the shank. For variations on this theme refer back to pages 31-33.

The next rig I can recommend is only a variation on the above, that is two Chum on two separate hairs. Beside the eye mounted piece, there will be another tied the same way, but to the bend of the hook. There will be times when you get confident takes on double baits, when swirls are greeted by the carp to single baits.

Some people have tried to make the attachment of the bait to the hook less time consuming and many ideas gave come to the fore. One, for instance, involves the use of pole elastic, of which a length is superglued to the shank of the hook; the length of this is quite short. What you have to do is pierce, say a piece of Chum, with one of those **'Nut Drills'** that Kevin Nash makes. Once you have made this small hole, put a baiting needle through it and catch the pole elastic and drag it back through the Chum. Once through, secure it with a boilie stop or similar. Because of the tension of the elastic, the Chum is held tightly against the hook shank.

One I favour is something I have been playing about with of late. It again involves the use of pole elastic, but this time the elastic is fashioned into a loop. How you achieve this is simple. First pierce the pole elastic with the hook point then slide it round the bend of the hook over the barb, then pierce the elastic

The moment of truth.

again about ³/₈" away and repeat the operation. What you'll end up with is a loop of elastic about the size of a piece of Chum. Now carefully manipulate the pole elastic into position - about halfway along the shank - make sure it forms a perfect circle. Once completed, superglue. The advantage of this system is that it allows very easy and quick change of the bait. All you need to do is slip a bait into the loop and then, as I have found out, manipulate the Chum so that you find a 'flat' side, lay this so that it lies against the back of the hook. I have found that this makes sure the hooking arrangement, and the way in which the hook lies, are just right. I came to design this not just for the hooking capability, but for the ease of bait mounting. Tests seem to prove its effectiveness and again, this coming season, I will be trying it again.

This kind of development in rigs will continue, so keep your eyes on the carp magazines like 'Carp Fisher' and 'Carpworld'.

I do think that all our work on developing end rigs for floater fishing are sometimes coming at the problem from the wrong direction. I still believe that you can have success in either the quiet stalking approach or getting your fish to the point of 'competitive feeding', through careful baiting and not casting out until their defence of what might, or might not, be danger, is at its lowest ebb. This I know is often easier said than done but, for me, it provides a way round any special defence mechanism the carp may have built up by being caught a few times on the top.

TACKLE: THE BASICS
Brian Skoyles

The tackle you use for floater fishing will vary, depending on the type of swim being fished. Much of the time it's also down to what you feel comfortable with. Ask ten anglers what the best range of gear is for a specific situation and you could well get ten different answers. Whatever you pick, in terms of tackle, it needs to fulfil three criteria:

(1)   Can the gear selected present a bait correctly?

(2)   Does it give the maximum chance of landing the fish when it's hooked?

(3)   Am I being fair to the fish (hooking a fish in tangles of branches etc., on heavy gear, when I've no chance of landing them, isn't on).

Let's look at the three criteria mentioned above a little more closely. In one walk around a lake you could be faced with fish in open water that just might take a floater drifted to them on light line. Thirty yards on, you might have a couple of fish in a large bed of lilies, that might look at a bait lowered to them. Later still, you might see some fish on the fringes of some overhanging trees. Will they take a bait suspended from one of the outermost twigs?

So overall, I would suggest that the tackle you need for floater fishing must allow you to be two things:

(a)   Versatile

(b)   Mobile

Bearing all the above in mind, the following is a summary of my thoughts on tackle at the moment.

RODS

If you accept that it is important to have balanced tackle, that is, a rod, reel, line and hook that complement each other, I would be hard pressed to find one rod that will be ideally suited for all surface fishing situations.

I have, in fact, got five rods which I use almost exclusively for surface fishing or stalking, although, in truth, this is perhaps a little over the top.

My top five (sorry about the pun) are:

(1) **12ft Tricast L/R 3-8 1¼lb TC**

I'm not quite sure what this rod was designed for (feeder fishing, light

The author in all his floater fishing glory.

ledger, or what), but it's perfect for light line surface fishing. It's got the backbone to cast fairly heavy controllers a long way, but still takes on a good battle curve with lines in the 5 or 6lb range, plus the 12ft length is an advantage when mending line as it drifts over the surface. I've used this rod for several seasons now for a variety of open water situations, landing fish to well over 20lb. I rate it very highly

(2) **North Western (Carbon Kevlar) 12ft Multi-Range**

This is as near a general purpose rod as I've ever used, and it complements the 12ft Tricast perfectly. For the slightly heavier lines and longer range controllers, it's perfect. 7, 8 or 9lb line suits this rod very well. It has the backbone to help steer fish through soft weed at range, but is soft enough to hook and hold fish close in. At a push you can use lines a bit heavier than already mentioned, perhaps up to 12lb or so, but to me the rod becomes a little bit spongy in the hit and hold situations that normally call for the heavier lines.

(3) 11ft Glass 2¼ S/U Bruce & Walker Mk. 4

This is a beautiful rod to use. A perfect hit and hold rod, using heavier lines 11+lb. I think you would struggle to get hold of one nowadays, but if you ever get the chance, grab it; they are a pleasure to play fish on. Soft, with a through action that lets the rod do the work rather than the hook hold. I use this rod with lines from 11lb to 22lb

It allows you to stop fish and turn them away from snags safely. At a slide show I gave I was challenged over using such heavy lines; the question being along the lines that did I think it right to use brute force to drag fish through snags, out of trees etc. I stressed that I don't and I don't advocate anyone else doing it. The use of a strong but forgiving rod with heavy lines means you can stop fish becoming snagged without tearing hookholds. I'm convinced this is kinder than trying to free tethered fish on lighter set-ups. It's all a matter of balanced gear.

(4) 10ft North Western 1½lb T/C Glass Carp

An 'oldie but goodie'. I think you can still get these; they are perfect for situations where the water is relatively snag-free, but the banks are overgrown (overhanging trees etc).

Combined with lines of about 8-10lb, fished close in, they are a joy to play fish on. Soft and responsive, but not for the faint-hearted as you'll feel every lunge and turn.

(5) 6-9ft 2lb+ T/C Stalker

This is a conversion job. Some swims are very tight in terms of vegetation on the bankside. A soft action stalking rod is ideal in these situations. Mine's an old bass rod with the butt section cut down to 2ft - just sufficient to make the handle.

SUMMARY ON RODS

I said at the beginning that I cannot think of one rod that will be perfect for all situations. Perhaps your best bet is to think about the style of fishing you will do most, and cater for that. If you're just starting up and you're not sure, the nearest you will get to a rod for all occasions would probably be around 11ft long, test curve 2lbish, with a reasonably soft action. (Very little of my surface fishing is at long range).

REELS

I am currently using three models in various combinations with the rods already mentioned.

(1) Mitchell 300

A very reliable, robust reel. The gearing in these reels is straight-forward and built to last. In hit and hold situations with the heavier lines, they will not let you down. I've had mine since the late 60's and trust them completely.

The major disadvantage is that they are no longer trendy. You might be told that the bail arms aren't reliable and, in truth, this can be the one problem with these reels, but keep the spring housing clean and replace the spring once a year (a very easy job) and you'll have no problems.

(2) **Cardinal 55 (ABU)**

Another very reliable reel. I use a 55 for much of my medium breaking strain work. I like the line lay and the rear clutch adjustment. These are no longer in production but can be obtained second-hand. A very good general purpose reel that has served me well for many seasons.

(3) **Aero Bait Runner GT 3500**

Up to last year I used a Mitchell 410A for the lighter end of my floater fishing; it had super line-lay and good reliability. Over the past 12 months or so, I've been using the Aero Bait Runner GT 3500. It's a brilliant reel and I've been totally impressed so far. The advantages are three fold:

(a) Excellent line-lay - very important with lighter lines.

(b) The baitrunner facility - gone are the days of bruised knuckles.This facility is very useful when you need to tuck the rod under the arm or lay it down so that you can catty some baits out etc.

(c) A reliable rear clutch - a big plus over the Mitchell with a spool set clutch.

LINES

I know of no one brand of line that is best for all situations, so I tend to carry several spare spools loaded with different breaking strains of different brands.

LIGHTER BREAKING STRAINS

5lb Drennan Float Fish - I switched to this two seasons ago and I've been very impressed. It lies on the spool well, floats well, has a good knot strength and lasts well. I use it a lot in open water light line situations.

6lb Brent or Golden Marlin - These two lines are both very reliable, general purpose lines. Brown in colour, they lie on the spool well and knot well. They don't float too well, so often need treating if you want to drift baits around.

MEDIUM BREAKING STRAINS

8lb Golden Marlin or 9lb Brent - As mentioned above, very reliable, general purpose lines. The Golden Marlin in particular seems very good in weed. Several of the waters I fish have a weed problem, stringy rough stuff that catches over your line as you are playing a fish. This stuff can rough your line up very badly and Golden Marlin tends to be very good in this situation, plus it's cheap enough to change regularly.

HEAVIER BREAKING STRAINS

11lb Sylcast, 11lb Brent, 12lb Golden Marlin - I'm happy to use any of the above. They are totally reliable in all respects.

18 or 22lb Maxima - In the heavier breaking strains this seems less springy and more controllable than most of the other brands. Having said that, I still pre-stretch it a little by playing a gatepost or two before I actually fish with it, otherwise it has a mind of its own and springs off the spool at the most inopportune moments.

To cover most eventualities I would normally take with me either a Cardinal 55 or a Mitchell 300 with spare spools of 18, 22lb Maxima and 11lb Brent, plus an Aero with spools of 6, 9lb Golden Marlin and 5lb Drennan Float Fisher. So, with two reels and four spare spools I can cover a full range of fishing possibilities.

HOOKS

Again, with such a wide range of possible fishing situations you will need a range of hooks to match the lines you might be using. It is most important that you get this right. A heavy hook on the end of light line is almost as much of a disaster as a fine wire hook on the end of 22lb Maxima. On the one hand you'll almost certainly lose the fish as the hook opens out and, on the other, you'll probably not get the take in the first place.

I use three patterns of hook for the bulk of my floater fishing.

(1) LIGHT LINES, OPEN WATER, SMALL BAITS.

Drennan Specimen Crystal sizes 10 or 12 - I've used these hooks for several seasons now and rate them very highly. They sit below a small bait such as a mixer or similar and hardly effect its movement at all. They also give a good hookhold, important in this situation as it can take a fair while to land a fish on this type of gear.

I wouldn't use this hook for any situation involving hit and hold, or lines over 6lb. It's a very good design for what it's intended for, but it is fine wire and therefore cannot be expected to cope with the stronger lines.

Stalking Tackle.

(2) GENERAL PURPOSE - LINES UP TO 12LB.

Partridge 22 Record Breakers - In my opinion, a brilliant general purpose hook for this sort of fishing. I particularly like the relationship between gape and shank length. High carbon steel gives it a good level of strength and, again, I'm happy with the hookhold this hook gives. Usual sizes - 6 or 8.

(3) HEAVY LINES.

Au Lion D'Or Extra Strong Spade (C1540) - For me there is only one hook for this situation and the Au Lion D'Or is perfect. You can tow cars out of ditches with this one. If you can't do it already, you will need to learn to tie a decent spade end knot but the effort will be worth it. This is a very thick wired hook which at first sight might seem off putting but, believe me, I've caught hundreds of fish using this pattern and I have complete faith in it. Usual sizes 4's or 6's.

There are many other good hooks on the market and, again, it's really a case of finding what suits you best; as a general rule I try to use the biggest and strongest I can get away with. This usually means I have to carry a fair range of patterns and sizes with me, but that's not a problem. A small fly box will enable you to carry a dozen or so different patterns or sizes of hook easily, with very little wastage of space.

TACKLE -The Business End.

Having acquired the necessary rods, reels, lines etc., the next question has to be - how am I going to present my bait to the fish? This means we need to look closely at the business end of our tackle.

Today there are many different rig bits, controllers, etc., available, some very good, some next to useless. The following is my thinking at the moment.

I have, over many years of watching carp, come to the conclusion that, in the majority of cases, it is important to try to make your hook bait behave and look as much like a free bait as possible. To this end I carry a range of controllers, rig bits etc. At times I'll need to speed a bait up, drift it up to some pads or swing it under some overhanging branches. No one rig will do all these jobs, so be prepared to be adaptable. I can put upwards of a dozen rig variations together from the various bits and pieces carried in a single, small plastic box.

Now, to the actual rigs:

Controllers to slow a bait down.

It is very rare to fish on a day where there is no wind at all and, on many days, the reverse will be true and you'll be floater fishing in quite windy conditions.

If this is the case it can present some problems of presentation. A wind in your face can present problems of keeping a tight line and a hookbait that ends up at your feet in no time at all. (Diagram 1).

DIAGRAM 1

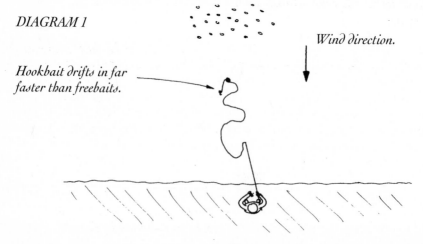

Wind direction.

Hookbait drifts in far faster than freebaits.

A cross wind can be even worse, with the wind catching both the line and the controller, causing a bow in the line and a drag on the bait that moves it in a totally different direction to any free baits. (Diagram 2).

DIAGRAM 2

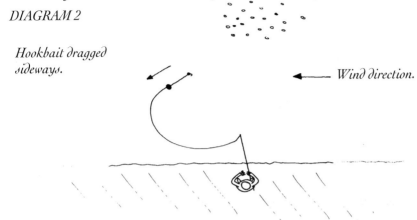

Hookbait dragged sideways.

Wind direction.

In these sort of situations, a controller that helps slow a bait down and does not catch the wind can be the difference between a take and a blank. There are several on sale, or you can make your own.

(1) Terry Eustace Floater Floats - A float with the weight well down in the water and it can help make a take easier to see.

(2) Gardner Self Cocking Controller - Torpedo shaped in clear plastic.

(3) Kevin Nash Controller - Slim and compact.

(4) Drennan Controller - Another torpedo shaped, clear plastic controller.

The main point to bear in mind when looking for a controller of this kind is that it should have the majority of its bulk sub-surface and little above the surface to catch the wind. (Diagram 3).

DIAGRAM 3

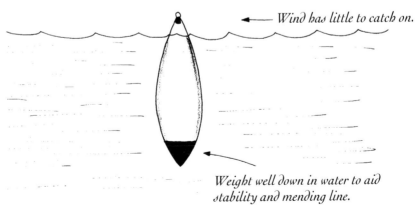

Wind has little to catch on.

Weight well down in water to aid stability and mending line.

I have, for many years, advocated a design of my own for this type of fishing and I have described it in print on several occasions (see Tim's book 'Carp Fishing'). Very briefly, it consists of two pike pilot floats glued to a cane stem, at the top of which is a small eye (whipped in) and at the bottom, sufficient lead wire coiled round and glued in place to sink the float halfway down the top pilot float. (Diagram 4).

DIAGRAM 4

I like these a lot, for several reasons.

1.   They are very stable - you can make the cane stem quite long, 8-9 inches being normal, longer for rough conditions.

2.   They are cheap and easy to make so it's no problem to make a range of sizes to suit a variety of conditions.

3.   They make relatively little disturbance on the cast and aren't too 'splashy' on the retrieve.

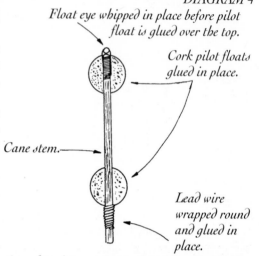

Float eye whipped in place before pilot float is glued over the top.

Cork pilot floats glued in place.

Cane stem.

Lead wire wrapped round and glued in place.

Using all the controllers mentioned in this section is simplicity itself. I just thread the reel line through the top eye or swivel and tie on a stop swivel. The hooklength can then be tied to the other end of the stop swivel. The length of the hooklength can be varied to suit conditions and the state of the fish (are they spooky or not?). Usually I fish a hooklength between 4 and 6 feet.

If you want to fish this as a bolt controller, a float stop can be positioned on the main line before tying on the stop swivel and then slid down to lock the controller in place. I would not advocate tying the main line and the hooklength to the top of the controller. It might sound like a good idea but if, for some reason or other, you crack off, or the fish becomes snagged and your main line snaps, the fish is left to tow the controller about or, worse, the whole lot, fish and all, becomes entangled in weed, trees, etc.

One minor problem with the set up described in (5a) is that the weight of the swivel can pull line through the controller and start to sink. I overcome this by using a small piece of tubing forced over the swivel, leaving approximately $\frac{1}{2}$ inch extending down the hooklength. Into this I push a small length of cocktail stick. This does three things:

(a) It stops the swivel sinking.

(b) It protects all the knots and helps cushion the cast.

(c) It acts like a small anti-tangle rig.

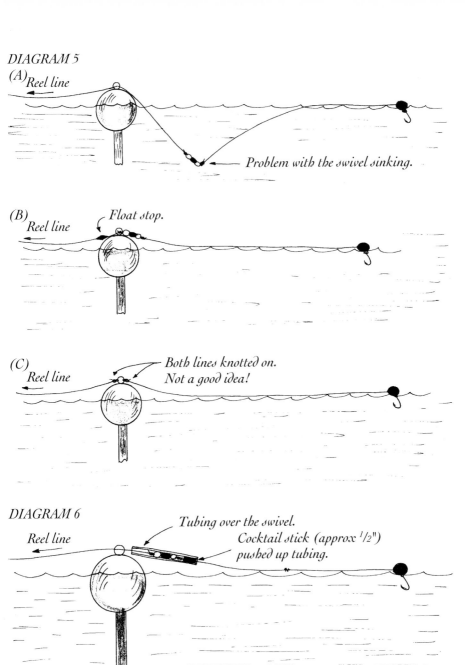

DIAGRAM 5

(A) *Reel line*

Problem with the swivel sinking.

(B) *Reel line*

Float stop.

(C) *Reel line*

Both lines knotted on.
Not a good idea!

DIAGRAM 6

Reel line

Tubing over the swivel.
Cocktail stick (approx $^1/_2$")
pushed up tubing.

The above set up will serve you well for most open water situations where there is wind drift to contend with.

Normally, I would start with the free running set up and watch the line for signs of a take. If the fish are proving difficult, I would add the stop to the main line to try to make the fish bolt.

Controllers to make a bait move or drift.

These are my favourite situations. A gentle drift towards reeds, trees, lilies, whatever; a nice, steady stream of free baits, but how to present the hook bait?

In this case we need a controller that can utilise the wind and catch it as much as possible to drag a bait into position. I know of no really good commercial controllers to do this job, but it is easy to make your own. Again, I have described these in detail in print before (again Tim's book, 'Carp Fishing'). I use two styles:

(1) The Branch Controller.

This is very easy to make. After the next winter gales, have a look around for some small branches, anything between ½ inch and 1 inch in diameter. Cut these into suitable lengths, anything from 1 inch to 3 inches I would suggest. Carefully drill these out with a drill to give a tight fit on any suitable tube. Most tackle shops sell stiff rig tube about ⅛ inch in diameter. (Old Biro centres are also very good). Rough up the outside of the plastic tube and Araldite it into the piece of branch. It's as easy as that. You now have a very natural controller that will not scare the fish, will lie flat on the surface and drift about under trees etc., wherever you want it to go.

(2) The Balsa Controller.

This is made by shaping 1 inch diameter balsa wood into a torpedo shape, then carefully cut it in half and inserting a tube with some lead wire wrapped round it, before gluing up the two halves of balsa and painting in as natural a wood effect as possible.

Why go to all the bother? By varying the amount of lead wire inserted in these types of controller, you can vary the amount of controller available above the surface to catch the wind. This can give you a tremendous range, in terms of how fast or how slow you want to make the hook bait move.

The rig is very simple to tie up; just thread the main line through the controller, tie the hook on to the end, set the controller to the length away from the hook you require

The Branch Controller.

DIAGRAM 8

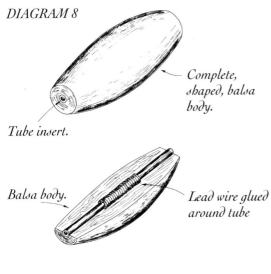

Complete, shaped, balsa body.

Tube insert.

Balsa body.

Lead wire glued around tube

and stop it in place, either with a small cocktail stick insert or a float stop.

A slight modification in the above might be of interest. The above rig is very efficient for close range work. If the controller is fairly heavy however, it does not work so well as it is very difficult to stop the controller from sliding up the line to the cast. If you use too tight a stop, it can damage the main line; too light a stop and after the cast, you're fishing a $1/4$ inch hooklink. Neither is desirable.

The modification I use is as follows. When I make the controller, instead of trimming

Cocktail stick insert or float stop.

the tube insert off flush with the balsa, I leave it sticking out approximately $1/2$ inch, then when I tie the rig up, I thread the main line through the controller and then also thread approximately 1 inch of soft silicon tubing on the line. I then tie the swivel on the end and add the hook length on the other end. The silicon tubing is then slid over the $1/2$ inch of tubing and over the swivel. (See diagram on next page).

I have total confidence in this drift/bolt set up. It's very simple to set up, works very efficiently, very rarely tangles and very rarely spooks the fish.

If you don't like to, or cannot, make tackle, you can achieve almost the same effect with some of the ET or Drennan pike floats.

DIAGRAM 10

Silicon tubing pushed onto controller tubing.

Swivel in tubing.

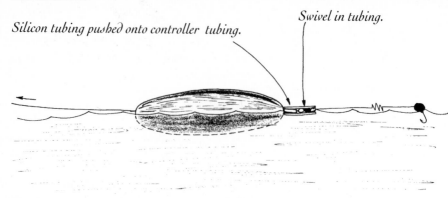

Controllers to help place a bait in or near weed.

Weed that does not reach the surface causes the floater angler few problems in terms of presenting a hook bait to the fish. The drift type controllers are particularly suitable for this type of fishing.

Weed that does reach the surface, leaving some clear patches alternating with denser growth, calls for a totally different approach, the main problem being that often you cannot drift a bait to the fish because it becomes trapped by the weed before it arrives where you want it. For this type of situation I usually prefer to put the controller at the end of the line and position the bait by lowering it into the water and moving the top rod about.

I have one favourite controller for this and you can make twenty or more of them in less than half an hour for a cost of about 10p.

End of the line branch controller.

All you need is some more of the small branches blown down in a gale and a packet of DIY 'U' shaped staples. Just cut the branch into the required number of pieces (I vary the size to give me a range of different casting weights) and then hammer a staple into one end. End of story - controller finished!

Tying up this rig is a little more complicated than those previously described, but hopefully Diagram 12 makes it reasonably clear.

First, slide a swivel up the main line, followed by a stop of some kind (Biro tube and cocktail stick, float stop, stop knot and bead, whatever system you prefer). Slide this stop up the line approximately 12 inches and tie the hook on the end, then take a length of line and tie it to the swivel. Cut this line to the length you require and then tie on the controller.

The beauty of this system is that a controller can be overcast, allowed to catch in the denser weed, then the bait can be gently lowered to the unsuspecting fish.

DIAGRAM 11 - 12 *(below)*

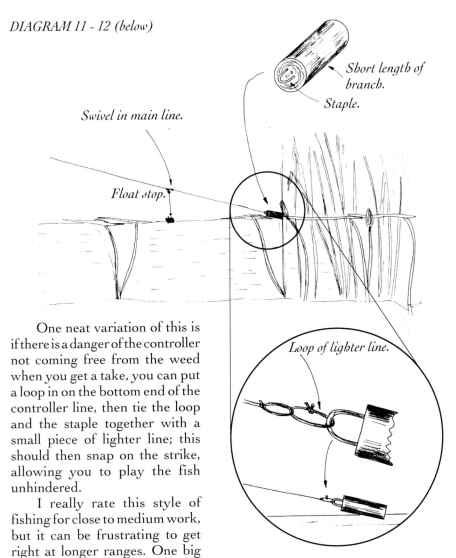

Short length of branch.

Staple.

Swivel in main line.

Float stop.

Loop of lighter line.

One neat variation of this is if there is a danger of the controller not coming free from the weed when you get a take, you can put a loop in on the bottom end of the controller line, then tie the loop and the staple together with a small piece of lighter line; this should then snap on the strike, allowing you to play the fish unhindered.

I really rate this style of fishing for close to medium work, but it can be frustrating to get right at longer ranges. One big plus is that you can get it set up and then lift the rod top a little, lifting the bait out of the water. This means that you can wait until a fish is nearby before lowering a fresh bait near it, thus avoiding the problem of a bait becoming too soggy and falling off the hook before a fish finds it. This is also a superb rig for fishing into the night with. Set it up before the light starts to fail, put a few free offerings round it, put the baitrunner on or use a buzzer, sit back and wait for the water to erupt. This system can also be used to present the bait very effectively close to trees and overhanging reeds etc.

Diagram 13

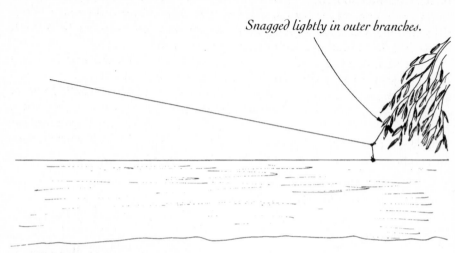

Snagged lightly in outer branches.

If you do try this, can I make a plea that you always put a lighter loop next to the controller - we don't want to be leaving line hanging from the trees on the strike! In practice, what usually happens is the lighter loop snaps and the controller falls into the water to be retrieved later.

Fishing at longer range - anchored rigs.

At times, because of angling pressure, wind direction, whatever, the fish can be feeding a fair way from where you can fish from. If this is the case it can become necessary for you to anchor a bait at range. I used to have several variations of rigs for anchored work, but over the last season I have been using a new gadget that has proved very efficient. It's also easy to make.

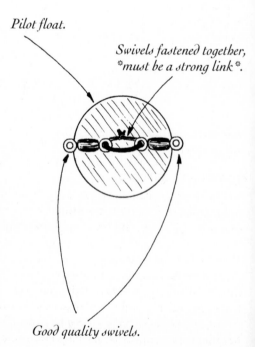

Pilot float.

Swivels fastened together, *must be a strong link*.

Good quality swivels.

All you have to do is to acquire some different diameters of pike pilot floats. Cut them in half; take two good quality swivels and fix them together (it is very important that you do this very strongly - I use stainless steel wire), then glue the two halves of the pilot float back together, trapping the swivels in the middle so that one end of each swivel just sticks out.

The rig is very easy to tie up, but you need to be very careful with the knots (see Diagram 14B), particularly the one to the lead. Just slide a stop and a small bead up the main line, slide on the controller, add a small length of tubing, then carefully tie on the lead, sliding the tubing down over the knot to protect it. Tie on the required hook length, set the stop to approximately one foot over the depth of water, bait on, and away you go. With appropriate rods and reels I've seen this rig used effectively at 90 yards plus.

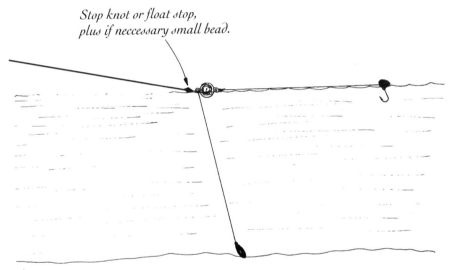

Stop knot or float stop,
plus if neccessary small bead.

Diagram 14B

OTHER RIGS.

The rigs already described serve me for most of my floater fishing, but two others are well worth a mention. One is my own idea and one I wish **was** my own idea! Firstly, the one I wish was my own idea:

The Beachcaster Rig.

As far as I know, this rig was developed for use in the Midlands by anglers faced with the problem of fish well and truly hammered on traditional baits. On these fairly shallow, well stocked waters, it was to prove very effective. The principle is to have a very buoyant float anchored in position, with a rod held high (almost vertical). The hook bait is above the float and the main line

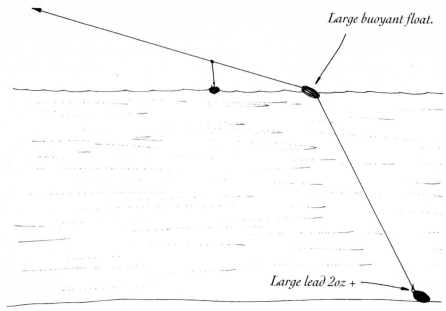

Large buoyant float.

Large lead 2oz +

Diagram 15
The Beachcaster Rig

can be adjusted to allow the bait to just rest on the surface.

It has several obvious advantages:

(a) It keeps the line off the surface - less chance of spooking the fish.
(b) Hooks can be relatively large as they are above the bait.
(c) Relatively heavy lines can be used.
(d) Not affected by weather - once in position, it stays there.

I must admit, I struggle with the Beachcaster Rig, but that's probably because it doesn't really suit my style of wandering about, drifting bait to fish etc. Having said that, many swear by it and it's a very clever rig, devastatingly effective in the right situation.

Secondly, the one that, as far as I know, is my own idea. It's a rig that I rate for night fishing - yes, night fishing. I've caught many carp off the top during the night but it does present some different problems, the largest of which is that you cannot see what you are doing.

The Night Rig.

This is only suitable for fishing the margins but this isn't a problem for me as I'm confident that carp come in very close after dark, if not before.

The idea is that just before dark the rod is positioned on two rests (buzzer and bobbin if you wish), so that the rod tip is directly over the position where you want the bait to be lowered. Two small controllers (small pilot floats) are then slid up the line and stopped lightly with short lengths of cocktail stick. The whole lot is finished off by tying the hook onto the bottom then adjusting

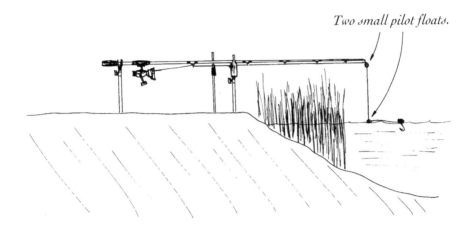

Two small pilot floats.

Diagram 16
the two pilot floats so that the top one gives you the height of the rod tip from the water and the bottom one is just clear of the surface but its weight helps keep the bait in place.

I tend to set this up before dark, leave it out of the water, just putting some free baits in position and then I sit back and listen. If I hear carp taking the free baits, I just put on a hook bait and gently lower it down. If I don't hear carp taking, I can either just forget it and concentrate on my bottom rods or I can put a bait out in the hope of fish moving in during the night using the buzzer to wake me up.

So that's my run down on rigs. What, in my opinion, are the other essentials of floater fishing? Looking through my gear, these are the things I wouldn't be without.

BINOCULARS.

Binoculars are an essential. They can help you spot fish; you can watch how they are reacting to your bait; I've even, on occasions, helped to time the strike holding the rod in one hand and the bins in the other.

I've recently acquired a pair of the mini binoculars; mine are Jessop 10 x 25 and they are brilliant, small, light, with very good optics. I wouldn't be without them.

Polaroids.

Another essential. Taking the glare off the water and easing eye strain from the sun. Ordinary sun glasses are next to useless. Try not to get the dark lenses, your aim is to cut down on the glare, not reduce the light. I use Optix HLT's. Not cheap, but very good for the floater angler.

Silly Hat.

I don't think it's silly, but everyone else does. The one I've got is the marines type thing with a large peak. Combine this with the Polaroids and you've got good visibility without the glare sneaking over the top etc. Highly recommended, even though friends give you the stick.

Bait Bag.

I was given one of these several years ago and thought it was a waste of money and a bit of a joke. Who needs a shoulder bag? The answer is, I do. It's a simple, no frills bag but it keeps pre-soaked mixers etc., in good condition and holds a few bits and pieces so I can go stalking without any effort.

Catty.

A reliable catapult is a must as often, accurate loose feeding is essential for good floater fishing. I prefer to feed in small doses, so most of the time I use the Drennan Mini Pult.

Landing Net.

For this style of fishing you need a compact, easy to use, landing net - none of the 50 inch arms with a North Sea trawl net underneath it. My floater fishing net has 36 inch arms with a standard, fairly shallow North Western net.

One final essential:
Mucilin or ET line floatant.

I never go fishing without this little tin of line floatant. No matter what brand of line I am using, from time to time I might want to make it more buoyant. This can help, particularly if I'm trying to drift baits near to trees etc. This tiny tin has helped me to catch many, many carp over the years and is an essential in my tackle box.

So, that's a run down on my basic floater gear. At first glance it might appear that it's a lot of gear to carry about when I suggest you should aim to be mobile. In fact, it's a lot more compact than you would think. Hopefully, the photograph of me, ready to wander off, illustrates the point.

All the basic tackle for the various rigs is in the larger bag; the bait and catty are in the smaller one. Rods are held together with the Velcro rod bands, plus the landing net. The spare spools are in the compartments of the bag; bins are around the neck, ready to use as I wander round.

That's it then, my basic tackle and rigs.

Just before we move on, three other things which could, or perhaps should, have been mentioned.

(1) A pacemaker or tranquillisers. Floater fishing can be exciting and

nerve-racking. It wouldn't be the first time I've had trouble holding the rod top still.

(2) A silencer for your shoes. If you are a noisy angler, this is an essential. Carp often take floaters right next to the bank, but not if you've just done an impression of the 1st Battalion Coldstream Guards. Walk quietly and slowly, you could be amazed how close the fish will feed.

(3) Sting-eze. The number of times I've become totally absorbed with watching the fish and it's taken me some time to realise that I'm knelt in a bed of nettles; or you hook a fish and grab hold of a bramble for balance. Sounds thick, but it happens. There again, perhaps it's me who's thick and it only happens to me!

Brian's methods work! Here he poses with a good twenty caught on one of his own floating baits.

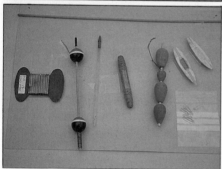

A selection of Controllers referred to:

1. *Home made variations*
2. *The making bits and pieces.*
3. *Branch, drifters and a mixer fixer.*
4. *Various commercially available
   controllers.*
5. *Dumbells.*

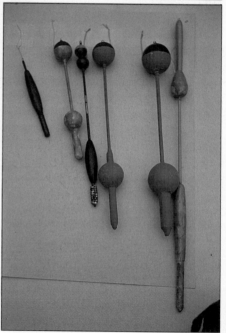

APPROACHES TO SMALL WATERS

Brian Skoyles

Right, you've arrived at your chosen venue; you've brought a range of gear and a variety of baits. How do you decide what to do?

First of all you should try to find out about the water, particularly its stocking and past fishing history. This knowledge is important before you actually start going walkabout around the lake. If the water has 15 carp in it and you locate 6 or so, it's a result, and probably worth pursuing. If the water has 200+ carp and you locate 6 or so, you'll probably keep looking to see if there are any better situations to exploit.

Equally, it is important to have an idea of the experience of the fish you are trying to catch. Pile a load of bait on top of battle weary fish and it could be the last you see of them for days. So, first off try to get a working knowledge of your water, then it's down to what you do on the day.

When I arrive at a water I usually spend a fair while having a look around. If it's a very small water, one or two acres for example, I'll often leave all the gear in the car and just polish up the Polaroids and wander slowly round the lake. It it's a bit bigger, I'll still wander round the lake but I'll take the basic stalking gear with me so I'm ready to drop in on any chance that comes my way. The problem with this however is that you can be tempted to start fishing for the first fish you see and miss on on another, perhaps easier, fishing situation.

As I am wandering about, I am considering three things:

(a) Holding areas.
(b) Wind effects.
(c) Problems.

Let's look at each on in detail:

(a) Holding Areas

To me, the definition of a holding area is one that the fish regularly want to spend time in. These areas can be natural ones such as overhanging trees, weedbeds, sun traps, or man-made - such as private banks.

Learn to recognise holding areas. They are often the most reliable source of action, particularly on more pressured waters.

(1) Trees.

Carp love to get under trees. Some days they'll spend hours hanging motionless under the branches. At other times they often swim from tree to tree along a margin, investigating food items, often only inches from the bank.

Carp love to get under trees....

70

Finding your carp is a vital ingredient in the successful floater fishing

How do you find out if they are there? I always spend a long time around trees when I am stalking fish. I try to position myself so I can look down through the branches but still see the open water nearby. For a while, I'll just sit and watch. If fish are present, it's time well spent. Are they looking for food or just having a rest in the shade? If looking for food, try to flick the odd bait in so you can see how they react. If they're just taking a rest from the rigours of the day, I'll often keep moving and return for another look later on. If I think I can do it without scaring the fish, I might leave them a few free offerings, preferably out in open water if there's a drift, so that they'll arrive naturally under the branches.

If no fish are present, but it's on a known patrol route, I'll often drop some baits in and just sit and wait for a while to see if any fish move in. This is often more productive that the first two options I've just mentioned as the fish move onto bait rather than bait moving onto fish, which can make them nervous on the more pressured waters.

Islands which have trees that overhang the water can be very productive, but knowing what's underneath can be harder to ascertain. Again, look for any disturbances, tell-tale rings or ripples in the water, and make good use of the binoculars. If conditions allow it, drift some free baits across and underneath and, again, wait to see if there's any reaction.

(2) Weedbeds.

Carp love weedbeds. They are an obvious food source, often trapping items blown about by the wind which, along with the natural food resident in the weed, make them very popular with cruising carp.

Always approach weedbeds with caution, fish often lie in the weeds with their backs actually out of the water. They can also be very close to the bank; one careless, noisy footstep can leave you with an explosion of water at your

feet, a racing heart and a missed chance.

Fish in weed are not always easy to spot. Try to position yourself so that you have a good overall view then just sit still and watch. You'll sometimes see odd stems twitch or a surface carpet of decaying weed lift as an unseen body below it changes direction. I have, on occasions, seen dorsal fins break surface or a tail gently fan the air.

If you find fish in these circumstances, do be in a hurry. These fish could be your best chance of the day. Often in weedbeds, as with under trees, fish can feel safer than in open water; they are more relaxed and therefore likely to inspect your bait. After all, in many cases it's looking for food that's brought them there.

You have one big problem though - how do you get free baits to the fish? You can't just throw the baits in as this will obviously scare the fish. Catty the baits into open water and, unless you have a strong, facing wind, they won't drift far enough in, being stopped by the outer weeds before they reach the fish. I know of no really effective solution to this problem. I tend to use a combination of ideas in the hope that between them, they will work.

One - I sit and watch until I am sure where the fish are and, as far as possible, the routes they are using through the weed, then I wait until the coast is clear, so to speak, and then carefully catty some baits in.

Two - I also put some baits in open water in the hope that some will drift at least part way in. This serves another purpose as well, in that if you are lucky, the fish moving about in the weed come across the baits further out and start to feed on them. If this happens, you are often onto a winner, as they are usually hungry fish in the right frame of mind.

If these alternatives aren't viable because it's either calm, or the fish aren't moving about much I have, in the past, resorted to a little bait dropper made out of a film canister. (Diagram 1). The idea is you very slowly lower it in with a few mixers etc., which float out as the canister turns over on its side. It's not very efficient, but at times it's the only way to get the baits into the weed without scaring the fish.

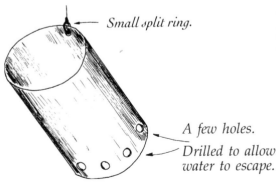

Small split ring.

A few holes.

Drilled to allow water to escape.

Weedbeds in open water can also be productive. Once again, look carefully, make full use of the bins and try to get some free offerings to drift in to see what happens. Much the same can be said about weedbeds up against areas of bank you cannot get to. Look, wait, and try to loose feed.

(3) Lilies.

In some ways, these present the same kind of problems as weedbeds in that it can take time to spot fish; it can prove difficult to place any quantity of free bait in the area without scaring the fish and you can scare fish before you have seen them if you approach the area carelessly. Having said that, lilies differ from weedbeds in one major respect. There is often a great deal of clear water underneath the broad leaves. Weed growth needs sunlight, the large; leaves prevent sunlight reaching the bottom of the lake therefore little or no weed grows. So you have a situation where you can look at an area of the lake and the whole surface can be totally covered with leaves (moorhens walking across the top without getting their feet wet, sort of thing), but under the surface it can be relatively clear and fish can move about fairly easily. These areas can be very productive for the floater angler, but how do you know if fish are present?

First of all you have to look for 'give aways' as I call them; that is, clues that indicate a fish is present. Carp are fairly broad fish and they cannot move past the roots without touching them and this usually makes the actual lily pad move in some way. It might just appear to vibrate, giving off tiny ripples in the process, or it might move slightly to one side then return to its original place. If the water is shallow, odd leaves might lift (sometimes called tenting). If you watch carefully, it's not unusual to be able to follow the path of a fish as it meanders about looking for food under the pads without actually seeing it at all.

In the above situation, if you can get some baits on or around the pads, it's amazing how good and, at times, how persistent the carp can be at finding food. I've seen fish push and push pads until they've reached a floater trapped in a dense confusion of leaves. These fish are very catchable because they have no chance of seeing the line etc. Having said that though, it's not fishing for the faint-hearted or ill-equipped.

(4) Safe Areas.

Most lakes have their popular swims which usually have anglers in them. Some lakes also have areas that are private or inaccessible for some reason. Whatever the reason, these situations can create holding areas.

In the first example, the holding area is likely to be as far away from the popular swims as you can get. When fish are cruising around on the top, they can obviously become aware of bankside movement, noise etc. They usually keep away from this and, as a result, can often be found tucked away in odd corners of the lake where a quiet approach can often spot some of the lake's population taking the sun or the shade, whichever takes their fancy. On the other hand, you might fish a very popular day ticket type water that has no quiet corners, just an angler every 30 to 40 yards or so. In this situation middle weedbeds or general open water tend to become the holding areas. Just be aware of the possibilities and react accordingly.

Private, inaccessible areas are a problem you can do nothing about, but at times it is possible to set a trap by baiting likely entrance and exit routes and just being patient.

(b) Effects of the wind.

For many, the ideal surface fishing conditions are hot, sunny and calm. I don't mind the hot and sunny, but I do like to have wind!! Not the sort that results from a night at the Indian, more the sort that opens up all kinds of possibilities with regard to moving fish about and drifting free offerings around.

(1) Moving fish about.

Over the years of watching fish on the top, I have often been surprised by how much water they cover. At times, this appears fairly random and therefore very difficult to predict, but at other times it is possible to move to an area before the fish arrive. For me, perhaps the most predictable of these is when you have a new wind or a wind change, particularly in summer.

Fish will often collect on the margin receiving the wind drift, or on the side of an island in the same situation. (Diagram 2).

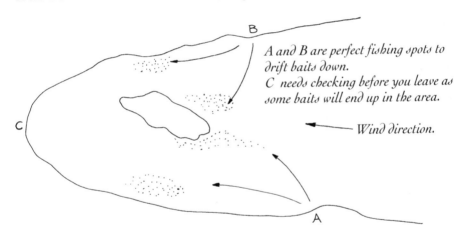

A and B are perfect fishing spots to drift baits down.
C needs checking before you leave as some baits will end up in the area.

Wind direction.

My ideal conditions would be a steady breeze pushing down a lake that, as evening approaches, starts to die away to a gentle ripple.

These conditions can often result in a fair number of the lake's inhabitants being around the margins and, as the wind dies, they can be particularly responsive to baits that are drifted down to them on the remnants of the breeze.

Once a wind has been blowing for some time, the advantage seems to become less, perhaps the undertow takes suspended food back up the lake a bit and the fish go with it.

One of my favourite sights when I'm floater fishing is the sight of a wind formed scum bed. A good, steady wind will free various dead and dying vegetation and drift it around the lake. In certain conditions, this will collect in the corners of a lake or between weedbeds. These can present perfect floater fishing conditions. Look at all the advantages; food has been collected and drifted to the same place; the old vegetation provides cover for the fish, the same vegetation allows you to approach without the fish seeing you and, lastly, you can use stronger line etc., than you normally could in open water situations, as the scum disguises it.

(2) Drifting free offerings about.

A good steady wind, predictable in its direction, can make certain floater situations brilliant. If you can provide the fish with a steady stream of free offerings and they can become preoccupied to the extent of losing their natural caution as they compete for food as it drifts to them. In these conditions, catching becomes easy and, even on relatively hard fished waters, multiple catches become possible on easy waters, large numbers of fish a distinct; possibility. My own personal best for numbers of fish goes to an evening session on a small two acre lake that produced eleven fish to high doubles, in just over three and a half hours.

My aim, in these conditions, is to find a peg upwind of where I've seen the fish, or expect them to be, then start to drift baits with the wind, basically increasing the quantity as the fish start to feed more avidly.

A steady, predictable wind can also be an asset in helping to drift baits under trees, into weedbeds etc. Again, position yourself downwind of the area you wish the fish to feed in and then allow the wind to do its work, providing the fish with a steady supply of food that generally they will react to.

One tip at this stage. Don't feed too heavily at first; better to introduce a few baits; let them drift about so you can check the course they take (it can be harder to predict the route than you think and it's infuriating if they drift off course and you end up with fish smacking down free offerings in an area you cannot get a bait to). It's also good policy from the point of view that you can watch and wait to see how the fish react to the bait. (More about fish reactions later).

(c) Problems.

Your best laid plans can be ruined by two main problems:

(1) Other wildlife
(2) Other anglers.

(1) Other Wildlife.

There have been many occasions when I've thought that the only good duck is one sitting in an oven with an extremely large orange stuffed up its rear end. I've also fallen out with various other feathered things, ranging from

swans through various gulls, coots, tufties, the odd Canada goose and anything else that flies, flaps, paddles and eats floating baits. On some waters they can be a real pain. In many cases it is the more popular fishing water where I'm sure half the wildfowl wouldn't know how to feed on their natural diet if their lives depended on it.

They create more problems than just eating the bait. For a start there is the spook factor. The number of times I've been creeping towards the margin fish-spotting, you slowly part the last few reeds – and come face to face with a mallard or two. All hell breaks loose, quacking and flapping, they charge off down the margin and the fish you were after explode in a vortex of spray as they head for waters distant. Nothing you can do about this one other than say "Oh dear!" and look for some other fish.

Another problem is, you arrive, catty some baits out then thirty seconds later the water is being churned to a froth as all the wildfowl on the lake lands and starts fighting over your free offerings. The answer to this one is look before you catty. On most waters the wildfowl will not come too close to you; even the most persistent duck thinks twice if it's going to be bopped on the beak with the tip ring of a stepped up Bruce and Walker. So basically if I look around and spot wildfowl, I then look around for situations where I can feed the margins. I also prop the landing net out in the open. Generally, in these situations, the fish don't seem to mind it as it's still, but it usually makes the wildfowl nervous and, in consequence, they stay that bit further away.

On heavily fished waters, wildfowl learn to associate angling with food so - and this sounds too simple to work - don't let them see you. I've often gained valuable extra minutes fishing by staying well back from the bank and only putting baits out when I'm as sure as I can be that the resident pests aren't within seeing or hearing range.

All in all, I don't think you'll ever solve the wildfowl situation but you can minimise the problem by fishing short whenever possible, not baiting up when they are about and staying out of sight if possible. Personally, I've never found leaping about etc., of any use; it might qualify you for a place in Jane Fonda's workout class but it rarely seems to impress the ducks. Likewise cattying stones etc.; most ducks seem to think it's free boilies etc., and it often attracts, rather than scares off.

(2) Other anglers.

This is a tricky area to write about as the aim is not to offend but to comment on a situation that exists.

If you decide to go walkabout and try to locate and then catch carp off the top, ideally you need peace and quiet. To be realistic, this is not always part of a carp fishing scene. It won't be the first time I've spent ages slowly getting into position to fish for the odd margin feeding fish to have them spooked by a visitor enquiring how things are going or, better still, making the observation "Did you see that whacker bow-waving out towards the middle, mate?"

The problems of other anglers not being aware of what you are trying to do is not easy to solve, plus the other angler has an equal right to be at the lake and, in most cases, it is a lack of understanding rather than someone deliberately mucking your fishing up. I often try to anticipate a problem before it occurs and if I'm stalking in pegs fairly close to other anglers, I often tell them before I start, what I'm trying to do. In most cases, other anglers take the hint and if curiosity gets the better of them, they usually approach quietly. If they don't, oh well, at least you are no worse off than you would have been. If I'm having a go at other anglers spoiling your (the stalker's) fishing then, in fairness, it can work the other way round and as you wander around you can also spoil other anglers' chances. So again, I often check with other anglers before I wander about. Something like "Will if disturb you if I have a wander about in the bay opposite?"

On small lakes, this sort of good manners can save a lot of hassle for all concerned. After all, in many cases it's possible to have anglers sitting on one bank and fishing near the other. Look at it from their point of view; they've spent eight or nine casts getting a bait under the trees, then half an hour later there's some clown peering through the trees lobbing mixers about. You wouldn't be over pleased either!

Summing Up.

This then would be my approach to a small water floater trip:

1.   Have a good look round - try not to be tempted to stop off at the first fish you see. You can usually thoroughly investigate all the options on a small lake in less than an hour, then it's back to the car, select the appropriate gear and give it a try.

2.   Don't be in a rush to get a bait in the water once you've decided on an area to be fished. Try to work out a logical approach to what's in front of you, how best to loose feed, any wildfowl problems, best place to fish from, etc.

3.   In many cases you won't usually be fishing from the well established pegs, so sort out the problems before you hook a fish. I remember once hooking a fish, playing it for a while and then realising that I couldn't get down to the water to land it. As a general rule, weigh up the odds and only present a bait

*Big fish from a
small water.*

to fish you genuinely believe you can land. This might seem a strange thing to say, but once you get into the stalking mode there will be times when you'll have fish feeding in very inaccessible places. It's not hard to get carried away and drop a bait onto a fish too close to a snag or too far under a tree, resulting in the inevitable crack off. Not good for you but, more important, not good for the carp.

4.　Be organised to deal with a fish once you've netted it if you are stalking and you want to keep the gear to a minimum. If sacks are allowed, I prefer to carry a sack rather than scales etc., then once the fish is netted, I can sack it before returning to the car for weigh sling, unhooking mat, scales, camera etc.

Feeding Techniques.

Throughout this section I've tried to put across my approach to small water floater fishing.

How you locate and then approach your fish is obviously important as I've tried to stress, but one other factor is also vital to success and that is how you feed the fish prior to presenting your hookbait.

In Carpworld 3 (Winter 88/89), I presented my thoughts on this area of floater fishing. I called the article I.R.S.L.I.P. and I couldn't leave any section on approaches to surface fishing without looking at this aspect of your approach in some detail.

Briefly, the article was called I.R.S.L.I.P. because the letters represented the stages that I felt carp went through in terms of reacting to a bait.

I - Indifference.
R - Response.
S - Sampling.
L - Limited Feeding.
I - Increased feeding.
P - Preoccupation.

Two years in, I'm still happy with the principles expressed in the article. Summarised, they are as follows:

Indifference　　Fish often ignore baits at first but if a consistent, steady supply of freebies is drifted over fish they eventually respond.

Response　This response takes many forms, from circling round, odd swirls near baits etc., before they try the odd one.

Sampling　Fish are aware of the baits and start to take the odd one, often tentatively, or with a lot of swirls. Often longish gaps between takes.

Limited feeding　Sampling increases with fish becoming more confident. Takes at this stage often settle down and become less splashy with the carp rising to the bait and sucking in smoothly.

Increased feeding　At this stage, fish start looking for baits and, after sinking one, will often keep their mouth near the surface as they turn towards the next nearest bait. It's not unusual, at this stage, for fish to take 10 or 12 baits or more in a continuous sequence.

Preoccupation   As it suggests, the carp has one thing on its mind - to mop up baits. It actively searches and competes for as many baits as possible.

My argument in the article was that it is often worth taking the time to feed an area, allowing the fish to progress at their own pace to the last two stages, the big advantage being that the chances of presenting a bait and having it taken **confidently** are greatly enhanced at these later stages.

So, for the vast majority of small water surface fishing:

1.   Take a good look round.
2.   Weigh up the options.
3.   Once an area, or group of fish is selected, take your time, feed carefully and regularly and don't be in a hurry to get the hookbait in the water.

Remember, an hour well spent before putting a hookbait on can be the difference between a confident take and a hooked fish, instead of a half chance and a spooked fish.

I would suggest there could be one exception to the above general rule and that is a very heavily pressured water where the fish are very wary. In this situation, it is often the case that any concentration of bait can make fish very nervous and, on occasions, cause fish to actually leave an area. This is where your research on the water can help. If I know a water has highly experienced fish, I often spend the first hour or so either watching a single freebie or even fishing a single hookbait. The bait is likely to be fairly large (a torn off chunk of floater cake for example).

It is possible that even a super shy fish will take that one chance out of curiosity before they become aware that it's a hookbait.

When surface fishing, you have one major advantage over the times you are bottom fishing, and that is you can see the fish and the bait. Capitalise on this advantage; get to know how fish react in various situations and fish accordingly.

A good friend of mine once said to me "You spend more time surface fishing than anyone I know, but actually have hookbaits in the water a lot less than most I know".

That observation sums up my approach; ten minutes in the right place at the right time is all you need, but you'll often need a lot longer to find the right time and the right place.

APPROACHING LARGE WATERS
Chris Ball

The whole approach to the larger waters that abound in this country means that you will be looking mainly at gravel pits in some shape or form.

It's this kind of fishing for carp that has, until only 10 years ago, been largely neglected. Not surprising really, because the thought of trying to tempt a carp that lives in acres and acres of water seems, on the face of it, almost impossible at times, but it's not. Floater fishing can break the back of waters like these if you can get the preparation right. That means doing your homework and using one of the most important parts of the whole operation in catching any carp, never mind just surface feeding carp. **Your eyes.** It sounds such an easy thing to say but, in my experience, lots of people who fish for carp don't use their eyes and so miss out on so many chances and the excitement that surface fishing offers.

When tackling large waters, I still spend 98% of my time walking, looking, watching and more walking. Why you might ask? Well, often you will be faced with the scenario I outlined at the start - huge gravel pits but with a light stocking of carp. If you try to approach this kind of water in a limited way, i.e. you fish the closest swim to the car park or the bank looks nice and flat, enabling your set up to look just right, you're heading for disaster. You might as well go sunbathing!

The carp will be in areas where they feel comfortable, or where there is food, or they might feel safe. Naturally, what you have to do is find these special places. It can be hard, and often hot, work in summer but in the end, the rewards outweigh any of these minor problems! Remember, carp are creatures of habit and can be vulnerable once you have penetrated their armour; only then can you make the most of it. I call this the 'ten second slot', for that tiny amount of time is all you need to present a bait to a huge fish, possibly your best ever.

That all said, where do you start?

If we imagine it is the close season and we have picked a good, bright, clear day towards the end of May; make sure you have your old fishing clothes on, be prepared to get dirty. Take a small tackle bag with you. In the bag will be binoculars, Polaroids, floaters (whatever), a catapult, pen and pencil and some bottom baits (boilies). I say boilies because don't think for one minute that life revolves solely around floater fishing, for when tackling waters like these, any chance must be acted upon immediately should one present itself, either on top or the bottom. Believe me, you'll kick yourself if, for instance, you find several good fish rooting about on the bottom and you are trying to either make your Chum sink or find yourself scratching at the ground looking for worms!

Naturally, the holding areas where carp tend to congregate, such as lily pads, snags (in whatever shape or form they may take), and weed beds are the areas to concentrate on. Climb trees, or try to get on higher ground whenever possible. Remember, the water may not be clear enough to see into to any great extent although, in fairness, our imaginary gravel pit will more than likely be clear, especially at this time of year. Look for any kind of movement in the water around these areas; concentrate, don't just look quickly, but study, wait, even sit down and watch the water for any kind of sign that something is displacing the water or an involuntary movement of a lily pad or a branch.

Sometimes the signs can be obvious, such as heavy swirls (especially when you approach an area), or a fish might disturb or spook another close by. Yet another sign that can often be observed is a shiny bump that signifies a carp's back or a dorsal fin that slowly waves just above the surface. I'm sure you have an idea of what I am getting at. The only way you will become proficient at this is to practise, for if you start with this approach in mind, I

Chris with a good 20 from Wraybury - a very large, difficult water. This floater caught fish was a reward for long periods of observation at the water, mainly during the close season.

promise that suddenly a whole new world will become apparent.

However, this water we are at today is unlikely to throw up a load of fish in the first place that you look into. A good starting point and an area of special interest, as a general guide, is to look in the place that's at the end of the wind on the given day. Again, if there are trees or high ground, get up there!

It is surprising how much a difference being just a few feet above ground can make; the reflected light off the surface of the water changes and with the additional help of Polaroid glasses, things can look so different. There have been times when I was sure that there were no fish in a given area, but finding just a small tree to climb revealed several very good carp lying motionless in heavy weed.

Looking at areas into which the wind is blowing is only a start and don't be surprised if there are no carp around. The point is, always look at all of these places, even if it means a long walk. If you do this often enough at some of the places I have mentioned, you will maybe stumble on a gold mine. That one chance to find a fish, or numbers of them, can be the one chance you need. In close season visits you can build up a picture of where fish are likely to be at a given time of the year or under certain conditions. This is only a guide of course, for carp are notorious for not conforming to any rules, but remember what I said earlier - they are creatures of habit and we can use this to our advantage.

Other main areas to look for are overhanging trees and bushes or fallen trees; I make mention of these as opposed to snags in the water for carp, by instinct, often congregate around these safe havens. Naturally snags are an important area to observe carp in.

Snags and weedbeds, natural carp haunts.

Imagine, if you can, that upon investigation, we have found several carp lying under a large overhanging bush, not just any bush, but one that you have, on several other occasions, spotted carp under. They may well be lying motionless just below the surface; try not to scare them. This takes practice for it's vital that you do not arouse them or put them on their guard because they won't feed or, worse still, may not appear in the area for some time afterwards. So, be as quiet as possible. This means your actions, as well as movements; try not to step on any pieces of branches or uneven stones. Something like this can catch you unawares and make for sudden movement which can be disastrous. If all is OK, the fish will not have noticed you and will continue to just lie there. Now is the time to try them out with some bait.

First tip, don't throw a handful of Chum straight in over their heads; as likely as not they will just scatter or, at best, slowly sink from view and then slowly melt away. You will find that even in still conditions there will be some kind of drift on the water; use this to your advantage, catapult just a few pieces close by. If these don't look like they are moving towards where the fish are lying, scatter some in the opposite direction - remember, not too many.

As an alternative to this, you can chance your arm and just drop, or flick, an odd piece out very close to the carp. I have found that you can get away with this without scaring the fish, but it's hit and miss. What can happen is that this solitary piece of bait will apparently be ignored for perhaps some time then, suddenly, a carp will either mouth at it from a distance (like trying to taste it without touching it) or, better still, any particular carp, not just the closest, will just sidle up and take it looking like he never had a trouble in the world! This has happened, and more than once, when I've been presented with four or five carp almost at my feet and just a few feet from my eyes.

Getting close to your quarry is so important. Only then can you see so much more in the way they look at a floating bait. Believe me, some individual carp consistently take a bait in a certain way. Let me explain. Often the same fish will take a bait almost without fuss and create no disturbance or, at the other end of the scale, another fish will be splashy and rush up to take before another carp beats it. But I digress, back to the fish we have found under the bush.

If, by luck, the bait we have thrown out does come close to any of these fish we have found, there is considerable advantage here for us insomuch as the fish see these potentially tasty items having arrived on the drift and they might well investigate. It may still take some time but I advise that you stick it out and watch what happens. This is the way to learn the habits of carp, what they are likely to do and, most importantly, their reaction to surface baits in general; how they might like one type of food more than another, for fish on some waters have different preferences to others. You can have a tremendous

Carp on some waters have different flavour preferences to those on others. Be prepared to experiment.

response on fruity flavour floater, or I've known oily fishy types of flavoured Chum to have the edge. The fact that you might well be faced with is that there will be no response from the fish even after a couple of hours. Leave them alone for the time being and carry on your walk around the lake. Now this might seem like giving up, and in a way it is, on these particular fish maybe. You will be amazed how carp can vary in their reaction, in the same water but in different areas.

The next place we approach is a corner of the lake that is unaffected by wind this day. Tucked away and quiet, it is covered with a form of algae and scum mixed with feather and blossom. This can be a favourite place for carp to lie or bask. Again, our approach is vital; be as quiet as possible. Because the surface area is covered with this 'gunge', it will offer concealment for us and obscurity for the carp. Throw out some bait to land on the edge of the 'gunge' before you start poking about looking for the carp. See if anything moves as the bait lands in the surface; it's an easy thing to spot, sometimes a blind man could not fail to notice as a carp suddenly bolts in fright, disturbed whilst he is having a nap. If no movement by any carp is detected, carefully move around the bank; if there is cover, like bushes or broken down saplings, all the better. Now here is an instance where you might find a carp close to the surface - remember that shiny bump on his back that I mentioned in the opening chapter? At first you might not spot it because it looks like a piece of old wood or clump of weed, but carefully look automatically for signs like this. You will get the hang of this kind of approach if you start as you mean to go on. Observe, be careful, make no sudden moves. Sit tight and let the carp betray its presence to you, not the other way round.

The baiting approach can be the same. Bait up just outside the area and wait on events. You might well be presented by a different set of circumstances and in these differing conditions the carp's reaction could be far more positive, with fish on the bait much quicker. Now go for it! When they have all but cleared up the freebies, get more out quickly, close to where the carp are. With luck, competitive feeding will start to take place and after some time the carp become so competitive that they are fighting for it. Now you can feed those carp until they have the bait coming out of the rear end so to speak! It is my experience, especially in the close season, that you can never overdo this kind of baiting. If will help condition your carp to the delights of surface food and put you in a strong position when the season starts.

If you find, after careful observation that there are no carp present, still put some bait in the area. In fact, put bait in all the likely looking spots you come across as we continue our journey around the water. Sometimes, on very big lakes, you may have to retrace your footsteps back to the car so that you can drive to another area of the water that is too far to walk! Now look again at all the areas you put bait in on your way back, for although it is fair to say that swans and other waterfowl may be more than a nuisance at times, you might be surprised to suddenly happen upon two or three big fish slobbering at that bait which you threw in several hours before. Be particular and nosy. If, for instance, there is no bait left where you thought you put some in, find out where it has gone; has it drifted close to the shore, or gone out of sight under some bankside foliage?

Talking of wildfowl, although they can be more of a problem on smaller waters (I'm sure Brian has a bit to say on this point, for they can be an absolute pain and sometimes make floater fishing almost impossible where they [the birds] can see what you [yes, **you**] are doing, and home in on the floaters), they can become just as much a potential danger on the larger waters, but not in the same way. I've found that in some cases our huge gravel pits do support a tremendous head of all kinds of things that bob about on the water's surface and look pretty. They are not used to seeing that many anglers about in general and they stay out of the way. The problem is the general public! They too often have access to these waters, like Wraysbury, that large gravel pit near Heathrow Airport that Leisure Sport control. Our dislike of these bait eating devils is not shared by your average dog walker who views these, sometimes bright looking, creatures as wonderful!

Throwing out bread in some form or another to the ducks can make them aware that human beings like them. They, of course, can't differentiate between me, the fisherman (the enemy) and the dog walker (the friend) but waving the landing net around usually does the trick. The problem that arises is when you have eventually found your big carp and close by is Mr. Coot. The last thing you can do then is to wave your landing net around. Have you noticed how bold they progressively become? It's at this point that things can become tense and they (Mr. Coot) could destroy this chance you might have. Maybe it seems I am going over the top on this subject, but with so much at stake at this stage, I find it difficult to see the coot's point of view!

But let us continue walking round our big gravel pit, for we are not yet finished. As we come round yet another bend in the bank, suddenly it becomes apparent that here is some shallower water, for gravel pits aren't just deep all over. The reason we know it is shallow is because there are several large lily beds with bright yellow coloured flowers. This is a major area to concentrate on. Better still, we can see that in amongst the lilies there are fallen branches and, by the look of them, they have been submerged for some time. If you watch this area again, subtle movements can be seen. Of course, they might not be carp; jack pike in particular tend to hang about in these areas, they are super sensitive to movement. Often you can't see them because they're small and almost non-moving - but enough of them. The most obvious way to find if there are carp about is to use your eyes, carefully. Carp love to bask in amongst lily pads. They tend to have company with them (other carp). The way they lie in lily pads can sometimes be amusing, for they tend to have their heads stuck under a lily pad itself. Useful that, for they can't see you but, make no mistake, they often know you are there! Others might be stationary for a while, then suddenly move off, often disturbing or rubbing against other carp as they go. They then take up a different position and all goes quiet again, only to repeat the procedure again a few minutes later. I've known them do this while in sunken branches as well. But here in the pads these 'restless' carp are the ones to watch for, for they are likely to investigate any floating food. Beside this, watch for any movement of the pads, should they move sideways, this way, that way, and even up ways! Also they can appear to shake or move more startlingly out of the way as the huge form of a big fish pushes the pads out of his way. All of these signs show you that carp are present. Although this is the close season, I would put some bait out and see what happens. When the season begins and a rod replaces the bag of bait in my hand, I might not. I'll explain later.

Now, although all this preparation in studying the water, its moods and the fish, is rewarding, remember, what we have just done is only one trip. I have made, in the course of one close season alone (as soon as the weather was good) upwards of 25 trips to check all of which we have been through in the last few pages. It can take many **years** before you can build up a good picture of what might happen and where those elusive carp might be under any set of circumstances. However, hard as it might sound, the rewards can be enormous, for this kind of fishing is make or break: it comes down to the 'ten second slot' I mentioned earlier, because **all** your hard work comes to the fore in just that amount of time. Getting the carp to accept the surface food in the close season makes for that chink in the armour we are looking for. I've witnessed sights which few anglers have seen when I've been out and about on these 'recce' trips for, make no mistake about it, I don't care how hard, indifferent or canny these big carp are that live in places like this, they can be made to display themselves and do things most carp anglers would find hard to believe, not only in the close season.

Try to imagine, if you can, eight carp, four of them over thirty pounds, racing around trying to find where the next piece of bait is. I witnessed this at Wraysbury a few years ago; I had them going for three days. Good job I'm an honest angler for in that time I could have hooked any of these fish, had I had a rod with me. I say this to remind myself never to consider it!

My addiction with this challenge, coupled with modern technology, has enabled me not only to view and record in my own memory these events but, with the advent of the modern 'camcorder' video camera (hand held) unit, it is possible to 'read back' these memories over and over again on your own television! Besides viewing these sometimes whopping great fish in detail on your TV, it gives an insight into which fish are 'goers' when it comes to surface food. Yes, it might sound crazy, but some are definitely more keen on surface baits than others. The mirrors are generally the ones that come up and have a look. I've found the commons to be sometimes indifferent in the extreme to surface food. They might rush round with the other fish, but rarely do they take a bait! You can identify individual fish easily, especially when you are up a tree or on high ground, looking down into clear water. Remember these fish because these are the ones we will be looking for once the fishing season gets under way.

There are large waters around that hold good stocks of carp where the location aspect is nowhere near as difficult. Here it is easier to find the carp in the first place, but the procedure will be the same. First find them, then don't disturb them, get some free bait out in the general area and finally sit and wait to find out how they will react. The situation is the same, although the results are often more startling.

These kind of waters don't have to be gravel pits, for I know of some of the big, windswept London Reservoirs that fall into this category of having good stocks of carp in them. The carp here can present a completely different set of circumstances, for often you will find them at range and baiting can be a real problem. The aforementioned wind that is inevitably present on most days, can be a bonus, for we are drifting the freebies out to where the fish are. Some kind of baitdropper can be useful, as is the use of PVA string and the new 'No Tangle' from Kryston to get bait out to where the fish are. In truth, I do not have that much experience in the more heavily stocked large waters. I would still recommend you try to find fish that are close to the bank and capitalise on these kinds of situation.

On these featureless, regular shaped waters, most carp fishermen look to long range fishing and ignore the margins. Also, carp men tend to stick to certain areas of the water and leave vast parts unexplored. Use your eyes, legs and brain. You might be surprised at just what you do find. People really don't do this, even after anglers like me, and others, have been telling them for years. Sooner or later, the message is going to get through, so in the meantime, don't tell me I am a lucky so and so, and have golden wotsits: I haven't, although I do get lucky now and then (also, you make your own luck).

Anyway, enough of me going on. Once explained how I go about assessing these big waters, let's go forward in time to when we can fish for these big carp, the wonderful 16th June! In recent years, the weather has been good, certainly warm, sometimes muggy and hot. The 16th June is also the time when you are most likely to get other anglers on the bank, in fact, the first two weeks are the busiest. After this, it usually peters out, with only a smattering of general anglers about with the odd carp man fishing on holiday for a week or so. Let's not run away with the idea that we might be the only ones who will be creeping about - some might read this book and think of

Big water biggie. This Savey mirror fell to Chris's floating bait during the summer of 1990.

having a go. In truth, it has become more noticeable in recent years; I run into the odd carp guy who, like me, is stalking. It has also come about because for some people, the thought of trying to get a swim at their local lake at the start of the season has turned into a nightmare. They too are trying to find some peace and quiet!

Now, with any luck, you will have found the fish in the weeks up to the start of the season and, hopefully, conditioned them to the delights of floaters. The two days previous to the start, I've usually been at the water nearly all day long, if possible, so this gives an up-to-date, spot on idea of location. It can happen like this but remember the old adage 'the rules in carp fishing are, there are no rules'.

One year, at a big fish water, I had virtually lived with the carp for weeks before the start of the season then, with just two days to go before the off, I lost them. I had become so sure of where they were, I had them almost waiting for me to arrive. However, unbelievably, when I looked for them with just two days to go, they were gone! Completely vanished. Worse still, I could not find them anywhere. It took 10 days before I managed to locate them and a further day before I got myself in a good position and got one to make a mistake. So never become too smug in your approach; the carp won't let you, they will keep you on your toes.

However, on this occasion, when we arrive at our imaginary gravel pit, the carp are still in the same general area. The main thing to do is not to panic. Easier said than done. Can you imagine the excitement and anticipation that has built up over the past few weeks, for big carp have been as keen as mustard to snap up the free offerings. All you have to do is **not** to screw it up. Once we have positioned ourselves and quickly set the tackle up and placed the landing net at the ready, take stock of the situation, for your mind will be working overtime and your eyes will never leave the water. It will be OK to 'catty' out some bait, because the weeks and weeks of work you have done in educating the carp to become accustomed to feeding on the surface is now about to come to fruition.

With a small group of big carp in front of you, seemingly ready to take your bait, it's a great temptation to cast in their midst almost straight away. But let's be crafty about this, because you are unlikely to have more than one chance at these fish (that's because once one is hooked, the rest will more than likely get out of the area sharpish). Put the free bait out and see what happens first. You will notice that some fish are far more keen on floaters than others; also some fish will look bigger than others. So why don't we kill two birds with one stone? It is the biggest fish that we want to go for. By now, some of our carp will be up to investigate the floaters. With luck, their reaction will be the same as on previous occasions, i.e. **they want it**. If you can wait long enough, single out the best fish. Is he taking any food? Is he a loner or in amongst other fish? The reason I want to know all this is because now my attention is focused solely on this one carp.

He's the one chance I want; the one fish I need to take the bait and, in all probability, the one carp I've been looking at the most during the previous weeks. Can we pull it off? Can we be that selective? Or am I living in cloud cuckoo land? The answer is, I know it can be done.

With hands now starting to shake, check the tackle and the end rig. Is the bait secure? The hooking arrangement correct? Where are the weed beds, the snags? Are there bankside obstacles that might cause a problem when we hook the fish? Is there anyone about? They might be useful if you run into trouble after you hook the fish. All these things go through your mind in a millisecond as the adrenalin pumps through your veins and your heart thumps hard inside your ears. You **can** make a mistake, a costly mistake; this bite could be one of only very few chances you'll get on the water this year.

The big fish is now taking the odd bits of bait, although he seems to be on the periphery area of where the other carp are. That's fine, maybe we can pick him off. In the first few hours of the season, the carp's defences are at their lowest and you will experience almost a naiveness on the carp's part. Now I've noticed he's moved just a little away from the rest; only a yard, but that's enough.

Big water monster. This incredible fish of 36lb was caught from Wraybury early in the season - on a floater!

Right, now we've sorted out our head, lets get fishing. Get ready to cast. The idea is to cast into the path of where that big fish is moving, but suddenly, he turns and comes close to another good fish. They rush together at one piece of floater; the bigger fish just makes it, turns away with a heavy swirl that rocks the whole area and this takes him again another few yards away.

Now here's our chance, but just as we prepare to cast, the big fish turns quickly again. He's looking for more bait, other fish are taking some floaters just to his left, but he is moving slowly, I **must** cast. Out goes the controller and bait, the first cast of the season. It lands just right, with hardly a ripple. The big fish has seen it, he's beginning to move right on line, we're going to get it right! With just a yard to go, he finds another piece of bait and takes it on the run. The next hit is ours, it must happen. He comes forward, rising slightly in the water, this **is** it, but then, in a split second, another fish has rushed in from the opposite direction. A flurry of spray, the line shoots tight **we're in**. The other fish scatter. Christ! There are carp shooting off in every direction except the one we are attached to. He is just wallowing on a tight line, and comes in easily close to the surface, but a heavy swirl sends him shooting off at speed. But we have the measure of him and, some ten minutes later, he dives into the waiting net...

All's well you might say, but long before he came near the net I caught a view of him. He is **not** the one we wanted; that other, smaller, fish had ultimately beaten him to the floater.

How can I be upset you ask! In truth, I am not, but in the following weeks my mind will be thinking over these events; will I meet that big fish again this season, or next year...ever?

I lie uneasy in bed the next few nights... I see that fish as I close my eyes each night... just coming ever closer to the baited hook...

A VERY NICE BONUS
Brian Skoyles.

Chris and I agreed that although the major aim of the book was to look at the technical aspects of floater fishing, it wouldn't be complete without a chapter recounting a session or two to try to give an insight into our overall approach and feeling for floater fishing.

I've sat here for what seems like hours now, trying to make a start and I'm struggling. I'm struggling because I can't decide which session to go over. Floater fishing has provided me with so many special moments that it's hard to pick which one to recount here; perhaps it would be easier to pick the phone up and suggest to Chris that we scrap the chapter.

Right, I've made my mind up and, as the title for this bit suggests, it was

a bonus fish, in that I shouldn't really have been fishing for it at the time I caught it.

One of the lakes I fish is a brilliant surface water; lots of opportunities for stalking and a good head of fish that like feeding on the top. It's got several islands on it and the fish regularly patrol round them. I was on a week's session and early on in the week the wind had been blowing gently from the south east between the main bank and one of the islands.

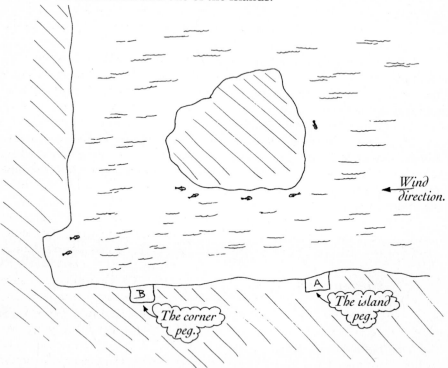

This had caused a good head of fish to collect in the bottom corner of the lake to the left of the island peg (A) and in front of the corner peg (B). Fortunately, the angling pressure on the water was light and I was able to sit in peg A, firing free baits across to the corner of the island, then it was just a matter of watching them drift between the island and the main bank and just a matter of time till the fish became well and truly preoccupied on the bait.

During the early part of the week, the wind was light, just rippling the surface, taking the baits very slowly to my left. As they reached the majority of the fish it was a fairly simple exercise to use a drift controller and present a hookbait in the same place, so I had a most enjoyable few days fishing further down the lake for the evening and night then visiting the floater area late morning and early afternoon. By the Thursday I'd had nine fish to 18lb+ from the area and was at peace with the world.

Friday saw a change in the weather. The wind strengthened considerably and I was helping to organise a Junior Fish-In on the water that weekend, so my floater fishing was over.

I spent the morning tidying up the bivvy and making preparations for the arrival of the juniors for the Fish-In. This I completed by lunchtime, much earlier than I expected so, with the first arrivals due at about 3.00 p.m., I had three hours to spare on my hands. It didn't take much thought to reach for the floater rods.

A short walk down the bank saw me standing above the island peg. Um, not as promising as previous days! For a start, the wind is much stronger and the extra ripple is making spotting fish much harder. I think I'll drop my gear here and fire out a few baits then slowly wander down to the corner to see what's what...

Those baits are pushing through fast; I'll be surprised if fish go to them. Still, let's have a look in the corner. I can see a couple of fish in the calmer water behind the island and I thought I saw one of the baits taken a couple of minutes ago, but I'm not sure. There's some big roach in here as well and it could have been one of these.

Neither of the fish near the island have moved to intercept the baits and the rest have collected against the bank to my left, much to the joy of a couple of noisy coots. At least they're not venturing out too far from the bank. I think I'll wander back to the island swim and have another look there.

Still nothing much. Hang on, I'll check with the bins but I'm pretty sure that a couple of fish are coming round the corner of the island. Yes. Not easy to see as they are a foot or so down, but definite fish and one is a good size.

Wonder if I can drift a bait to them? I'll try a cast past the corner of the island and see what happens. Perfect - about 10ft to the right and level with the corner of the island. No chance, that controller is dragging the hookbait through the water like it's fitted with a 10 horse power outboard. The wind's catching the line causing a bow in it and swinging the bait around and away from the side of the island. Shall I change rigs? I can't see the fish any more so I'll wander back down to the corner first.

Still no signs in the corner, just the same smug looking coots. Hang on, another pair of fish moving around the sides of the island, this time anti-clockwise, against the drift. I'll go back to the island peg to see if they keep coming.

Yes, here they come, slowly working their way along and round out of sight. Let's have a think. I've got a few fish moving around the sides of the island. A perfect wind for the bottom corner, fish should be stacked up there but they're not. I've got easy presentation at the bottom end but only coots feeding. Much harder presentation if I fish the island but at least I'll be near to what fish there are in the area at the moment. They seem pretty relaxed, just cruising in small groups. Because of the wind, feeding heavily will be tricky. Also it will be difficult to coincide a hookbait with freebies and cruising fish all in the same area at the same time. Plus, with all my wanderings back and forth, I've only got about an hour and a quarter left.

I think I'll opt for a single fixed bait in the obvious place, just off the corner of the island. At least that way there's minimum disturbance but a bait constantly near where a fish is likely to pass by.

Right, I'm set up. It's my usual anchored rig using the double swivel glued into a small pilot float, double mixer bait attached by a small hair through the knot of the hooklink.

A gentle cast, sink the line/baitrunner on, rod on the deck, one hand on the handle, the other holding the bins so I can watch the bait. Everything looks good; the wind has straightened out the hooklink and I can see my baits floating perfectly. Trouble is, I can't see any fish. Quick glance at the watch. 45 minutes then I must go to the car park to await the guests for the Fish-In.

Another check through the bins. Any signs? No. Oh well, it was worth a try. Hang on - fish coming round left to right, a group of three. I hope those baits haven't softened too much. First fish has gone past; second one…go on, go on…don't bother then; third one didn't even stop. What's the time? 5 minutes then I'll have to go. They're coming back straight towards the bait; come on, come on…big swirl, can't see the bait. Don't panic Brian, look at the reel line, it's picking up, baitrunner giving it big clicks, reel handle round - strike. Yes!

It's off down the side of the island. That's OK, no panic, it's fairly clear there. The only problems in this peg are at my feet. I've weed beds all along in front of me so I'm happy to play the fish further out so it's reasonably tired by the time it's close in.

It's stopped now and it's coming back along the island. Odd strands of weed on the line but nothing to worry about. Steady pressure, just let it stooge about. It's kiting left now towards the weed on this margin.

"Now then you noddy".

"Hello Bill".

That's good timing. Bill Cottam has arrived for the Fish-In with one of the lads (Kevin Green) just at the moment I've managed to weed up an obviously good fish.

I've had other fish in this weed earlier in the week and it's the soft clingy sort that doesn't damage the line but it can be a pain to bring fish through. I've found that good steady pressure tends to be best, plus lots of patience as the fish often just stays still for periods, but when it does swirl about it often frees itself, so that's the tactic. I'll try moving along the bank a little to get as near as I can to the fish, plus keeping steady pressure.

Yes, it's moving. Increase the pressure. It's coming - as a large clump of weed rises up in the water, plus a large tail that breaks the surface before going deep again. I'm going to give line again but I'm clear of the weed and back with a chance.

That's good, it's stopped and it's just going back and forth in open water again. It seems to be tiring - I know I am. I'll try a bit more pressure. That's good, it's on the top and coming nicely towards me.

" Any chance of a hand with the net Bill?"

Oh damn! It's back in the weed again. Nearly made it, but just at the last minute it got its head back in the weed, so it's stalemate again.

Same as before, steady pressure. Don't panic. I can feel it moving and I can see movement in the water so it's not too deep in the weed; just wait a bit. That's it, keep moving, come on. It's clear in front of me.

"All yours Bill".

Magic!!

Bite through the line and up to steps to some nice, smooth grass. Hook out and into the weigh sling. Just over 21lb. A few photographs then back you go.

Considering I didn't really rate the conditions and I didn't expect to have time anyhow, a very nice bonus fish.

Thank you very much.

A very nice bonus, fish – magic!!

SURFACE SUCCESS
Chris Ball

There is a large lake close to where I live; it's situated just on the Surrey/ Hampshire border. Surprisingly though, it has commanded little attention from carp anglers over the years.

However, the main interest and appeal which this place has comes from two sources, each of which have little to do with angling. The first is the British Army, the second, television! I'd better explain.

The land around this area belongs to the Ministry of Defence, as does most in the vicinity. The Royal Engineers live here and, as can be imagined, with the troubles afoot, security is high. Because of this, it's a wonder to me that we have not lost our access to this water, but the Army have a strong fishing club here so voices other than ours make sure we still can fish - for the time being anyway.

Television (BBC) used this backcloth to stage the occasional programme called 'Run the Gauntlet' which is usually on TV around Christmas time. The lake's setting is perfect, with its large open area of water and several interesting islands. It has its contestants running around doing all manner of 'action' things, including water sports and using amphibious vehicles. Being on Royal Engineers' property, so to speak, the 'props' are already to hand!

The land here is similar to other areas around these parts; sandy ground and heavily wooded - in this case, vast areas of pine trees. The general topography has little in the way of hills or any higher ground, so one gets the feeling of being out in the wide open air, if that's the way to explain it. Certainly, as you stand in one of the swims on the north bank and look out over the water, the far bank seems a long way off, although the water is broken up into manageable chunks by the islands, though these days they have been 'doctored' by the local sailing club - no doubt to give a clear view to check whether one of their 'fraternity' has tipped up or gone missing on the water.

This water has been in existence for many years, although it was originally man-made and still bears the mark of man's hand to this day. The most striking part of the lake's appearance is the wonderful rhododendron bushes that stretch around the greater part of the lake. In early summer they make for a colourful setting and add greatly to the lake's appeal. The water is not deep for most of the expanse, maybe 8ft in a number of places; generally you'll find 3/5ft.

Now, shallow water means weed and here things are no different. What sort of weed it is, I'm not sure, but it's tough and wiry. This, coupled with the water being, for most of the time, cloudy, makes spotting fish difficult but the carp do show themselves, either by leaping or some kind of disturbance on the surface.

The stocks of fish present can be divided into two types. First, the usual sort of general fish, tench, bream, roach, rudd, perch and pike. The second, guess what? That's right, carp but, here's the rub, not many. Although it is always a problem estimating the population of carp in large lakes such as these, captures seem to suggest less than **thirty** big carp live there. Work this out and you'll find that each of these carp has **two acres** to itself! Matters are made worse by the fact of the boating people, out in all the daylight hours **and** a motorboat that roars about the place, making sure all the budding 'Walter Raleigh' mariners are surviving! Oh, I forgot, water skiers are there as well. Now if all this sounds almost too much for you to contemplate, the final blow is the Army; what with night manoeuvres, amphibious crafts, divers (underwater) and squads of Army men always running about the place, it all adds up to something special. But this has to be borne because there are some cracking carp in there. They are from the original Leney strain, long, lean fighting machines with beautiful scaling, averaging around the 25lb mark.

It's now some years since several of we carp anglers became interested in this most demanding water. It was the time of the 'tiger nut' phenomenon and we decided that this was the way we were going to attack the water. We found that there was an area into which the carp came frequently; it was a bay. This was also comparatively quiet to the activities of the non-angling public, although fishing after 10.00 a.m. was hit and miss. I found that from first light to 9.30 a.m. offered the best chance of a run. Our little band of anglers managed to land several of these prized carp as the fish became used to finding bait in our heavily baited areas, but it was tough going with a fish only coming every now and then. It was during one of these early morning sessions that a breakthrough came for me that was to have far reaching effects in the years to come.

The morning had become hot again as I sat, half hidden in the rhododendrons; little had happened. However, far out in the lake, over to the right, just at first light, a big fish had jumped. Even though that carp had jumped some 150 yards away, the ripples came over to me and broke the mirror-like surface. I wondered what fish it might be. How big was it? And was it going to come anywhere near my bed of bait? All, however, was quiet.

I fell asleep as the sun came up and the day burst forth in all its glory. It was the muffled noise, some time later, of a boat being launched that made me stir and shake my head. Good grief, it was nearly 9.00 a.m.; I'd been nodding, on and off, for nearly 80 minutes. A breeze had sprung up and the lake now looked so different, more hostile, than the hushed dawn of a few hours before. But now as I looked out into the distance, I could see the vague forms of Army personnel alighting onto the water. Time was running out, time to call it a day - on this water anyway. Thoughts were already on another lake I was off to; I had a day off from work. Great life if you can get it!

Hanging on until the last minute of fishing time is something I've now done for years, for often a chance has come in these last few minutes. Now standing by the rods, just supported by the front rod rest, everything else packed away, I carefully scanned the water just in case any movement was evident.

Of course, just as I was fiddling about in the tackle bag and not looking at the water, suddenly a heavy splash occurred over to the right, tight to the rhododendrons. This was well into the bay and in a place I have never seen a big fish move. That's interesting and, as I looked, crash! - he did it again! It looked a good fish as he hung there, standing almost on his tail before entering the water, almost in slow motion. These moments with carp are one of the great attractions of the fish, it can make the hair on your neck bristle and your mouth go suddenly dry. With this occurrence, I quickly reeled in the rods, checking that the baits had not been interfered with. I decided I'd have a look at the spot where the big carp had jumped - after I'd been back to the car and packed everything away. Could I get anywhere near to the water at that point? I'd investigate.

Besides some tiger nuts, I picked up a bag of Chum Mixer, just in case. I had not, until this point, actively thought of surface baits as a means to catch one of these fish. Saying that, I always have thoughts of the surface on my mind. With some people it's women, with me it's surface feeding carp! Just call me old fashioned! When I looked at this particular part of the lake I noticed a kind of path that led into the rhododendrons at this point. Where did it lead? I had to find out. To my dismay, after only 10 yards or so it seemed to finish but wait, looking further at this spot I could see a tunnel in the rhododendrons. Maybe, I thought, this was used by the Army whilst on 'combat trials' or just mischievous boys making a 'camp' here in the summer holidays. I made up my mind to have a look.

Once inside this tunnel, the available light was cut by 50% and the floor of the path was covered by a layer of dead leaves. Not the sort that crunch noisily under foot, but allowed you silent passage. The water was only a few feet away to my left. It's a strange thing, but it seemed to be almost illuminated, with the light cut out by the overhanging rhododendrons, the bright light penetrating from the outside producing this weird effect.

There was just enough room to allow access along this route as I made my way. After 20 yards, I stopped, thinking it must be close to where that fish jumped. At this point I pushed through the tough rhododendron branches and peered into the water.

There was no mistaking the shape of **five** big carp lying just a few feet from my eyes! I froze, caught my breath and slowly got into a crouching position. The nearest fish to the bank was so close to the surface that his back was out of the water and he looked unconcerned as we watched one another, almost eyeball to eyeball! This was a tremendous looking fish, very long (at least 30in) and displayed that Leney speciality that some of these fish had. It was a linear carp - having mirror scales of the same size, perfectly along the lateral line. He was just opening and closing his mouth and looked like he would be a prime candidate of a piece of Chum. But, enough of him, the other four carp present were beauties as well; every one looked over twenty pounds and, on first inspection, none looked any larger than another.

After this, several of the fish moved around the general area and it was clear that one in particular was that much bigger. In practice, when you look at fish in the water, if one looks a bit bigger, you can bet, when landed, that fish would be a good deal heavier. So this carp could be an upper twenty. All the big carp present were mirrors and were in super condition; one came right in close to the bank, almost under my feet. He was different though, paler than the rest and displayed a high back and greater depth. He must be around mid-twenties.

This time spent looking at the fish sounds like it might have taken some time; in truth, this took but a few minutes. I moved back and reached down into the bag of Chum. What should I do? I decided to throw some in over to the right as there was a ripple coming in from right to left. The Chum scattered over an area as it hit the branches on the way down to the water, but soon several pieces were coming in on the drift, just right. Any moment now they would come into vision of the linear and the pale coloured mirror. One piece in particular arrived right over the mouth of the linear. What would he do? He never moved; didn't even cock his eye upwards. Another couple of bits came close to the other carp, again no reaction.

I threw some more out. Let's see what happens this time. Suddenly, there was a swirl. The first batch of Chum had become lodged against some branches. The linear was at the Chum, then the other mirror was by his side, up he came as well, another piece gone. That's it. Where's my rod?

Easier said than done. I tried to extract myself from the clinging branches, never giving myself enough time. I caught my T shirt and ripped it, but soon I was back in the tunnel and travelling back towards the open area. Once there, I started to half run, half walk back to the car. After a hasty tackle up and checking that everything was in order, it was back into the tunnel.

I must explain that both rod and landing net were broken down. This was a great aid as I tried to squeeze myself, plus the tackle, along this tight passageway. Once back at the place where the fish were, I quickly checked they were still there. They were, although their position had changed, in fact into a slightly more open part of the bank.

Up went the rod - the bait was already in position - and after much struggling, I got the landing net in the right place. As explained, this area was tight, but not that tight. I figured a hooked fish would shoot out under the 'canopy' into clearer, deeper water. If I was strong and firm I felt that I could manhandle the fish back under the 'canopy' and into the waiting net.

Getting into position, I was pleased to find that my antics had not aroused the carp, so all was well. There was no Chum left, so very carefully I flicked out half a dozen, using just my thumb. These again, came down in the ripple, but as they came near to three of the carp, I now had dangling, just off the rod tip, my hookbait. This was it, the half chance I needed. The linear spotted the Chum, he moved slightly forward, a piece disappeared. Shakily I dropped the hookbait close, next to this fish. He ignored it at first but turned just as another carp accelerated from the left and they both shot forward together. It seemed they were on a collision course and the hookbait was in the middle! A fraction of a second later, an almighty wrench on the rod tip. I'm in!

What happened in those first few seconds was a blur, but I thrust the rod tip under the water immediately, the ancient Mitchell reel begrudgingly giving line just at the last moment, saving the day. The fish twisted and turned on a short line right on the edge of the 'canopy'. He hung there, out of reach. Time almost stood still, my mind racing at what to do next. The net, the one with the small throat to it, was half man-handled into place. In one hair-raising moment, the fish slid sideways over the net. That was the moment, the moment I remember even now as I relate this tale to you. For a minute or so I couldn't move; the old heart was pumping like fury and the head became swimmy, but as I came back into focus I managed to drag the net and fish up on to the bank. It was a big fish, the depth was really impressive and had me guessing that maybe here was a 25lb carp.

To cut a long story short, I managed to get me, the fish, net and all, back into an open area. There he was accurately weighed and turned the scales at 23lb 8oz. Upon inspection, he proved to be the carp that was the paler one; he was lightly scaled but totally unmarked with a great big mouth. Now I had the yardstick I knew there and then that the slightly larger looking fish must have weighed 5lb heavier.

This 'chink in the armour' in carp behaviour - the under the rhododendrons swim - has proved to be a winner as time has gone on and, even this year (five years on), I am still having success in this area of the lake.

So there you have a surface success story that, hopefully, demonstrates that the most important thing you need, and one of the main aids to carp catching you must use, is your **eyes**.

Good luck.

POSTSCRIPT

Long after the dust settled, the book had been written, the pictures and the drawings submitted, and we had started production an excited phone call from Chris was followed by the letter that follows!....

Dear Tim,

Well, what a way to end my season - in fact, the last day - and at Minley, a water I never really thought of fishing in the winter anyway. Who would? Christ, it's difficult enough in the summer.

However, never tell me that luck, fate, or whatever, doesn't come into play in our fishing lives.

There we were on Monday (Jan, me and Andy), ready to end the season at 'Willow', then when I asked John Raison, the owner, if I could bring Jan as a guest, he said "we couldn't fish because of a match". As Andy was off to France that evening he said if he couldn't fish locally he would more than likely knock it on the head. Maybe Broadwater, I said, but still he wasn't keen; then Jan said "How about a day at Send?" - but somehow I didn't fancy that either.

So, with the weather looking mild, on Tuesday evening I wondered, as I sat here in the Carproom, if those carp at Minley might be under the rhododendrons. When I looked on Wednesday afternoon - right on the road - there they were, at least four different ones, including two good 'uns. I got them to take Chum after a while and one fish, which looked twentyish, I hooked, but the hook pulled in a flash, unfortunately. However, within twenty minutes a mirror stormed up and took the Chum on the run! I got him in, spot on 18lb, a beauty. Returning the following day, but with conditions much cooler, I looked in the same place; there were several around. However, this time they were swimming much deeper, none came up for any surface bait.

I thought, there and then, 'I'll go and have a look at Cutt Mill', but as I walked back down the road to the car I thought I'd have a quick look in another spot where I knew they'd often be in the summer. There were three big, black shapes in the water; I scattered some Chum in the general area and soon, two of the fish present were 'having a go' - but only when it had drifted out of position!

Then one fish, between 15-20lb, showed an interest in the hookbait. I had to lift it off the water - **twice!** - to stop hooking him. This was because I could see the other fish - which was taking - was larger, although it never looked 30lb+. This larger fish would not come into the more open area that I had the hookbait placed in.

Eventually, of course, he did. No hesitation, up he came, down the hatch went the Chum! The usual form, held on a tight line, he just thrashed around on the surface. Quick as a flash I bundled him in the net...

Always sounds easy when you say it that quick! You can imagine what this experience is like - Hairy!!!

It was quite dark under the bushes (rhody's don't drop their leaves). When I looked in the net I thought, 'that'll do, that looks a very good fish'. Christ! I could hardly lift the net out from between the branches. I rang Andy on my portable phone (no jokes please) but he couldn't come, he was about to leave for France!

"How big?" asked Andy.

I looked down into the water, inside the net.

"Around 25lb" I said.

"Around 25lb" I said. It went 31,08 and might be the largest winter floater caught carp ever!

He rang off, saying he'd contact the Anglers' Mail. By now I'd cut the line and, with much effort, managed to lift the whole lot out of the water onto the bank. Only then did it dawn on me that here was something special.

Special? Bloody hell, it was a monster! A magical Leney linear, with proportions the like of which I haven't seen since the days of Frensham! 34" to the fork of the tail, 36¼" to the tip and a girth of 26". **At 31.08 it might be the largest winter floater caught carp ever!**

Well, there you have it, a nice tale to end the season with...

Good this fishing game!

Kind regards,

Chris

For other titles in the Carp in Depth series see inside back cover